DIGITAL ACTS OF WAR: EVOLVING THE CYBERSECURITY CONVERSATION

JOINT HEARING

BEFORE THE

SUBCOMMITTEE ON INFORMATION TECHNOLOGY

AND THE

SUBCOMMITTEE ON NATIONAL SECURITY

OF THE

COMMITTEE ON OVERSIGHT AND GOVERNMENT REFORM HOUSE OF REPRESENTATIVES

ONE HUNDRED FOURTEENTH CONGRESS

SECOND SESSION

JULY 13, 2016

Serial No. 114–138

Printed for the use of the Committee on Oversight and Government Reform

Available via the World Wide Web: http://www.fdsys.gov
http://www.house.gov/reform

U.S. GOVERNMENT PUBLISHING OFFICE

25–510 PDF   WASHINGTON : 2017

For sale by the Superintendent of Documents, U.S. Government Publishing Office
Internet: bookstore.gpo.gov   Phone: toll free (866) 512–1800; DC area (202) 512–1800
Fax: (202) 512–2104   Mail: Stop IDCC, Washington, DC 20402–0001

CONTENTS

DIGITAL ACTS OF WAR: EVOLVING THE CYBERSECURITY CONVERSATION

Wednesday, July 13, 2016

House of Representatives,
Subcommittee on Information Technology, joint
with the Subcommittee on National Security,
Committee on Oversight and Government Reform,
Washington, D.C.

The subcommittees met, pursuant to call, at 1:06 p.m., in Room 2154, Rayburn House Office Building, Hon. Will Hurd [chairman of the Subcommittee on Information Technology] presiding.

Present from Subcommittee on Information Technology: Representatives Hurd, Blum, and Kelly.

Present from Subcommittee on National Security: Representatives DeSantis, Russell, Hice, Lynch, and Lieu.

Mr. HURD. The Subcommittee on Information Technology and the Subcommittee on National Security will come to order. Without objection, the chair is authorized to declare a recess at any time. We expect to be interrupted by a vote series later this afternoon, and because of that, we're going to be abbreviated in some of our opening statements.

I appreciate you all being here today. Cybersecurity isn't a buzzword anymore. It's real. And you all's written statements were helpful in helping me better understand this issue, and if we're able to get a whole-of-government talking about this and making sure that we're all singing off the same page, I think we're going to be safer as a Nation. And I appreciate such a distinguished group of folks joining us here today.

And with that, I'm going to yield to Mr. Lynch for his opening remarks.

Mr. LYNCH. Thank you, Mr. Chairman. I would like to thank Chairman DeSantis, as well, and all the members of the subcommittee on both sides of the aisle. This is an incredibly important topic, and I appreciate the all-star panel that we have here today to help us with our work.

I understand that certain questions that might be raised today in this forum are best left for a more secure setting if we're going to get into any detail, and so we know that at the outset. To this end, I appreciate the willingness of our administration witnesses to conduct a classified briefing for committee members at a date to be yet determined. So thank you.

As underscored by National Intelligence Director James Clapper in his most recent Worldwide Threat Assessment of the U.S. Intelligence Community, continuous innovation in cyber information technology has been accompanied by the emergence of new and complex national security threats. According to Director Clapper, and this is a quote, "Devices, designed and fielded with minimal security requirements and testing, and an ever-increasing complexity of networks, could lead to widespread vulnerabilities in civilian infrastructures and U.S. Government systems."

These lapses in cybersecurity are highly susceptible to exploitation by a range of threat sources, including foreign governments, such as Russia, China, North Korea, and Iran, who are motivated by cyber espionage. There is also the threat of cyberterrorism perpetrated by terrorist groups designed to promote online recruitment, propaganda, and financing activity, and incite lone wolf attacks.

The SITE Intelligence Group reports that the Islamic State actually maintains its own so-called Hacking Division, or United Cyber Caliphate, a group of prominent hackers that has already published several kill lists of U.S. military personnel online. Moreover, hackers have repeatedly targeted the U.S. commercial sector for illegal monetary gain and money laundering.

The continuous onslaught of massive data breaches in the public and private sectors here in the United States and worldwide evidences the complexity, diversity, and far-reaching implications of these cyber attacks. Our national security and cybersecurity framework must be equipped to prevent and mitigate against public sector attacks, such as the critical breaches of information technology systems at the Office of Personnel Management back in 2015. These cyber attacks not only compromised the personal identifiable information of over 22 million individuals, including their Social Security numbers; rather, as noted by FBI Director James Comey, "They also yielded a treasure trove of information about everybody who has worked for, tried to work for, or works for the United States Government."

The past few years have also witnessed breaches of computer systems at the State Department, the White House, the Internal Revenue Service, and the United States Postal Service, as well as reported leaking of sensitive information pertaining to employees at the Department of Homeland Security and the FBI.

At the same time, our cybersecurity defenses must be able to deter and respond to threats targeting private sector companies motivated by illicit financial gain. It's my understanding that the Federal Reserve is currently leading other U.S. regulators in developing baseline security safeguards for U.S. banks in the wake of a February 2016 attack in which cyber criminals successfully transferred $81 million out of the Bangladesh central bank to a casino in the Philippines.

We've also witnessed the infiltration of computer networks at JPMorgan Chase that compromised the account information of 83 million households and businesses; a $62 million breach at Home Depot that compromised an estimated 56 million payment cards; and multiple cyber attacks against the Target retail chain that resulted in the theft of approximately 40 million credit and debit card numbers and the personal information of up to 70 million customers.

Clearly, the national security threat posed by cyber attacks is multifaceted and demands the continual development of cybersecurity policies and countermeasures that are adaptable, modernized, and comprehensive. I look forward to discussing with our witnesses at today's hearing what steps we are taking in this regard.

Thank you, Mr. Chairman, and I yield back.

Mr. HURD. I'd like to thank the ranking member of the Subcommittee on National Security for his opening statement. And now I'd like to recognize my friend from the State of Florida, the chairman of the Subcommittee on National Security, Mr. DeSantis, for his opening remarks.

Mr. DESANTIS. Thank you, Mr. Chairman. I thank the witnesses. I'm not going to give a full statement in the interest of time. I'd like to hear from the witnesses and get as much done until we have votes. But I will say that this is a very, very important part of our national security challenges and strategy, and it's only going to continue to be something that's more prevalent.

So I appreciate the chairman calling the hearing, and I look forward to hearing from the witnesses. And I yield back.

Mr. HURD. One of the areas we all talk about when it comes to national security strategy is the four levers of national security: diplomatic, intelligence, military, and economic. And one of the reasons we composed this panel this way is because of that. And we have DOD here, State Department.

Thank you, Mr. Kanuck and General Alexander, for your previous time in the intelligence community and now also representing the commercial sector as well, and, Mr. Singer, your work in this effort. So I think it's going to be a great conversation, and it is something important that we need to do.

And we recognize that the intent is to not get into classified information here, but I think General Alexander said it best in his written statement, that, "Without much public discussion," I'm reading from his words, "of our basic cyber capabilities, particularly on offense, we face two major challenges: It is difficult to have a reasoned discussion of how we might respond—at least in the cyber domain—and it is that much harder to deter offensive actions by others." So I think having a public discourse is important in the larger strategy.

And what we will do is, we're going to recognize General Alexander for your opening remarks, and then we'll have Ranking Member Kelly deliver hers.

Actually, before we begin, we want to hold the record open for 5 days for members who would like to submit a written statement.

And now I would like to recognize our witnesses. I'm pleased to welcome Mr. Aaron Hughes, deputy assistant secretary for cyber policy at the U.S. Department of Defense. Mr. Chris Painter, coordinator for cyber issues at the U.S. Department of State. Had a long, illustrious career at the Department of Justice as well, and White House, NSC, you name it.

Mr. PAINTER. Thank you, Mr. Chairman.

Mr. HURD. General Keith Alexander, retired, CEO and president—he's a retired general, but now CEO and president of IronNet Cybersecurity, former head of the NSA, ran CYBERCOM as well. Mr. Sean Kanuck, counsel at Legal and Strategic Consulting Services and former national intelligence officer for cyber. And Mr. Peter Warren Singer, strategist and senior fellow at New America.

Welcome to you all. And pursuant to committee rules, all witnesses will be sworn in before they testify. So please rise and raise your right hand.

Do you solemnly swear or affirm the testimony you're about to give will be the truth, the whole truth, and nothing but the truth?

Thank you. Please be seated.

And let the record reflect that all witnesses answered in the affirmative.

In order to allow time for discussion, please limit your testimony to 5 minutes, and your entire written statement will be made as part of the record.

General Alexander, you're up first. You're now recognized for 5 minutes.

WITNESS STATEMENTS

STATEMENT OF KEITH ALEXANDER

Mr. ALEXANDER. Mr. Chairman, distinguished members of the committee, Mr. Chairman, Mr. Vice Chairman, Mr. Vice Chair, it's an honor and privilege to be here before this committee. I think what you're taking on is vital for our country. And it's also an honor and privilege to be here with my esteemed colleagues from the past. Aaron, I think we've all been together, and Peter and I were on a committee just a few months back. So it's an honor to be here.

I'm going to hit mine rather quick. I recognize the classification issues that you raised, Congressman. I know that it's important that we don't raise those in public. But I do think we have to have a debate. I'm not proposing any red lines anywhere. I'm proposing that we start the debate in an informed way, where you, Congress, the administration, and the American people can engage in how we're going to work in cybersecurity.

There has been a lot of effort in that area with what my colleagues, Chris and others have done, but I think we have to go further. I'm going to briefly hit the top issues that I see that our government and our country need to take on, especially when you look at what NATO is doing, now recognizing cyber as a domain of warfare. We need to be out in front.

And it reminds me, when Chris was in the Department of Justice back in the 1960s, he worked with McNamara, and if you think about McNamara's approach on the nuclear deterrence, can we come up with a strategy for cyber that's equal to that?

Congressman Lynch pointed out some great issues that we see every day in cyber, from Home Depot to Target to everything that's going on. Companies are being hammered. We passed legislation recently that helps the companies, commerce, and government work together. It's a step in the right direction. But much more needs to be done.

Look at the change in technology, what's going on today, how rapidly this is changing. And if you look at the projections for the

Internet of Things by 2020, there'll be 4 to 10 times as many devices on the Internet as there are people on the planet. This is a huge capability and a huge problem.

Now, when we look at, "So what are we going to do about it?" think about the threats that Mr. Lynch pointed out. Criminal activities in cyberspace are growing and continue to grow. This year the biggest growth will be in ransomware. I think we're going to see that come out, and this is going to be huge for our companies out there, especially the small and midsize who can't afford world class capabilities.

And so it really gets us to a point where we've had in other committee hearings, so what do we do, how do government and industry work together? What's the role of government, what's the role of industry, and how do we share?

I'm not going to give you my "you have to do it this way or this way," but I do think from where you sit in this institution, to help start that discussion and create what you think from congressional oversight you believe needs to be done. Some thoughts on that as we move forward.

Who's responsible for defending the Nation when we come under attack? If you think about Sony being attacked, Sony has no capability to fire back. In fact, if we think about Sony firing back, we quickly get to the realization that if Sony fires back, that could get us into a war on the Korean Peninsula. We don't want that to happen. That's an inherently government responsibility.

If it's a government responsibility, that means government needs to be able to fire back when appropriate, when the administration, the President and the Secretary, determine. We can't see what's happening. The government can't see what's happening to Sony in time to do that.

So the first thing is bridging that gap of sharing information between government and industry so that government can do its first job in defending our country. We've got to start that debate. It's been hampered by Snowden and others, but it's something that I think it's important for you and the rest of the administration to take on with our country and with our allies.

Second, if we get to a point where our country comes up with the right framework, what would we want to push NATO to set as theirs? And we, our country, developed the Internet. We're the ones who started this. We ought to lead in securing it and coming up with the McNamara approach for how we're going to defend and deter in the same space.

And so what I really think we need to do is start that discussion without any preconceived notions about where it will take us, but put the best minds in there and say: Here's what we want to do. We want to stop these types of attacks on our industry. We want to ensure that our allies have the same sense and purpose, especially where we have alliances, and that we're all in agreement.

And so from my perspective, Mr. Chairman, I'm glad that you've taken this on. I see I'm out of time, so I'll cease work there, and thank you very much.

[Prepared statement of Mr. Alexander follows:]

Prepared Statement of GEN (Ret) Keith B. Alexander[*]
on Digital Acts of War: Evolving the Cybersecurity Conversation
before the Subcommittees on Information Technology and National Security
of the Committee on Oversight and Government Reform

July 13, 2016

Chairman Hurd, Chairman DeSantis, Ranking Member Kelly, Ranking Member Lynch, and Members of the Committee: thank you for inviting me to discuss digital acts of war with you today, and specifically, to engage in a dialogue with this Committee about the rules, norms, and constructs regarding acceptable behavior in cyberspace.

I also want to thank both Chairman Hurd and Chairman DeSantis for playing a leading role in the House of Representatives on cybersecurity matters, including through efforts like Chairman Hurd's legislation on state and local cybersecurity, which passed the House late last year, as well as Chairman DeSantis's leadership in looking into the Office of Personnel Management hack last year. And I know both of you have terrific partners in the ranking members on both your subcommittees, with Ranking Member Kelly's efforts on federal IT acquisition reform and Ranking Member Lynch's work on the OPM investigation.

As members of these subcommittees well know, the key systems and networks that make up what we call colloquially refer to as "cyberspace" constitute a set of critical assets that enable communication, promote economic growth and prosperity, advance the cause of freedom globally, and help ensure our national security and that of our allies. At the same time, cyberspace, as we know it today, has also become a digital battleground where nation-states and their proxies, organized criminal groups, terrorists, hacktivists, and others seek to gain an advantage on one another, whether through surveillance and espionage, criminal activity, recruitment, planning, and incitement to attacks, and repression of free speech and expression. Increasingly, we recognize that while the benefits of global connectivity far outstrip the potential costs, our increased connectivity makes us more vulnerable, as individuals, as groups, and as a nation. As a result, we also increasingly realize that we must proactively take steps to protect ourselves, our information, and our critical assets from the vagaries of crime, theft, espionage, and, yes, potentially destructive activities. And, perhaps most importantly, we understand that the increased connectivity of networked devices to physical systems makes it more possible to create real-world effects through cyber activities.

The numbers on the dramatic growth and expansion of our network connectivity are clear: by 2020, it is expected that IP traffic on global communications networks will reach 2.3 zettabytes, or 95 times the volume of the entire global Internet in 2005.[1] And, as you all know, underlying technology in this area is also growing rapidly, with processing capacity doubling

---

[*] Gen. (Ret) Keith Alexander is the former Director of the National Security Agency and former Commander, United States Cyber Command. He currently serves as the President and CEO of IronNet Cybersecurity, a startup

[1] *See* Cisco, *The Zettabyte Era—Trends and Analysis* (June 2016) at 1, *available online at* <http://www.cisco.com/c/en/us/solutions/collateral/service-provider/visual-networking-index-vni/vni-hyperconnectivity-wp.pdf>; *see also* Cisco, *VNI Complete Forecasts Highlights Tool*, *available online at* <http://www.cisco.com/c/m/en_us/solutions/service-provider/vni-forecast-highlights.html>.

every two years under Moore's law.[2] This combined growth in technology and IP traffic will be accompanied by rapid growth in the sheer number of IP-connected devices, particularly given our move towards the Internet of Things (IoT). Cisco estimates that by 2020 there will be 26.3 billion networked devices, the equivalent of more than three IP-connected devices per person around the world.[3] Traffic from wireless and mobile devices will also account for two-thirds of all IP traffic by 2020,[4] and worldwide mobile Internet penetration is expected to reach more than 70% around the same timeframe.[5]

And while this expansion of technology and connectivity means that we can expect to reap tremendous social, economic, and political benefits, it also means the attack surface for bad actors to target our nation is likewise expanding. And while we are all also well aware of the huge threat posed to our economic security by the rampant theft of intellectual property from American private sector companies by nation-states and their proxies—constituting what I have previously described as the greatest transfer of wealth in human history—I want to highlight an even more troubling trend that began to take hold in the past four years: the emergence of actual destructive cyber attacks, where cyber or other systems, data, or capabilities are permanently destroyed.

In 2012, we saw a set of destructive cyber attacks conducted against Saudi Aramco and Qatari Ras Gas, an attack that resulted in over 30,000 computers being disabled at Saudi Aramco alone.[6] And in February 2014, we saw the first-ever publicly reported destructive cyber attack by a nation-state on U.S. soil, with Iran conducting a cyber attack on the Las Vegas Sands Corporation in February.[7] This was followed later that year, in November, by the North Korea's attack on Sony Pictures.[8] These attacks represent a particularly concerning trend because they demonstrate an expansion in significant cyber capabilities from nation-states like China and

---

[2] *See* Annie Sneed, *Moore's Law Keeps Going, Defying Expectations*, Scientific American (May 14, 2015) *available online at* <http://www.scientificamerican.com/article/moore-s-law-keeps-going-defying-expectations/>.

[3] *See Zettabyte Era*, n. 1 *supra* at 2.

[4] *See Zettabyte Era*, n. 1 *supra* at 2.

[5] *See* Internet Society, *Global Internet Report 2015*, at 9, *available online at* <http://www.internetsociety.org/globalinternetreport/assets/download/IS_web.pdf>.

[6] *See* Director of National Intelligence James R. Clapper, *Statement for the Record: Worldwide Threat Assessment of the US Intelligence Community 2013* at 1, Senate Select Committee on Intelligence (Mar. 12, 2013), *available online at* <https://www.dni.gov/files/documents/Intelligence%20Reports/2013%20ATA%20SFR%20for%20SSCI%2012%20 Mar%202013.pdf>; Kim Zetter, *Qatari Gas Company Hit With Virus in Wave of Attacks on Energy Companies* (Aug. 30, 2012), *available online at* <https://www.wired.com/2012/08/hack-attack-strikes-rasgas/>.

[7] *See* Director of National Intelligence James R. Clapper, *Opening Statement to Worldwide Threat Assessment Hearing*, Senate Armed Services Committee (Feb. 26, 2015), *available online at* <https://www.dni.gov/files/documents/2015%20WWTA%20As%20Delivered%20DNI%20Oral%20Statement.pdf> ("2014 saw, for the first-time, destructive cyber attacks carried out on U.S. soil by nation state entities, marked first by the Iranian attack on the Las Vegas Sands Casino a year ago this month and the North Korean attack against Sony in November. Although both of these nations have lesser technical capabilities in comparison to Russia and China, these destructive attacks demonstrate that Iran and North Korea are motivated and unpredictable cyber actors.")

[8] *Id.*

Russia whose actions are more constrained by external political and economic considerations, to nations that might be more inclined to act or at least may be more unpredictable in the nature and scope of their actions. They are also particularly concerning because the fact of the attacks—and our nation's relatively limited, if any response to them—lay bare the fact that we have no real strategy or doctrine for how to deal with such events, much less deter other nation-states from undertaking them.

In order to develop such strategies and doctrines, and perhaps most importantly, to effectively deter these type of actions, we first need to understand better what constitute acts of war in the cyber domain. The reality today is that while we can all easily imagine acts that regardless of where or how they are undertaken, whether in cyberspace or otherwise, would constitute acts of war—the more challenging part is determining where that line should be drawn in the hard cases. That is, while there are cyber attacks with consequences that would almost certainly fall within the parameters of what we would be prepared to call acts of war—for example, attacks that cause major loss of life, destruction or incapacitation of significant portions of key infrastructure, or even attacks that cause massive economic damage—there still remains an enormous gray area of hostile nation-state actions that might approach, and even cross, the line.

In part, the determination of what constitutes an act of war is a legal determination and has legal consequences. International law, including the U.N. Charter, seeks to define when a nation may act in self-defense and how the international community might respond to a breach of the peace.[9] Similarly, a determination by the NATO Alliance that a member-state has been attacked could trigger the collective defense commitment in Article V of the NATO Treaty.[10] Indeed, this issue is all the more pressing given NATO's increased focus on cyber defense and its ongoing recognition, since at least September 2014, that activities in cyberspace can potentially trigger Article V obligations.[11]

At the same time, however, we cannot ignore the political and moral aspects of determining what constitutes an act of war. Even if a nation suffers an "armed attack" under the meaning of the U.N. Charter, it may choose not to respond. And many argue that the right of

---

[9] *See* United Nations, *U.N. Charter* Ch. 7, Arts. 39, 41, 42 & 51, *available online at* <http://www.un.org/en/sections/un-charter/un-charter-full-text/index.html>.

[10] *See* North Atlantic Treaty Organization, *North Atlantic Treaty*, Arts. 4-5, *available online at* <http://www.nato.int/cps/en/natolive/official_texts_17120.htm>

[11] *See* North Atlantic Treaty Organization, Cyber Defence Pledge (July 8, 2016), available online at <http://www.nato.int/cps/en/natohq/official_texts_133177.htm> ("We reaffirm our national responsibility…to enhance the cyber defences of national infrastructures and networks, and our commitment to the indivisibility of Allied security and collective defence, in accordance with the Enhanced NATO Policy on Cyber Defence adopted in Wales."); *See* North Atlantic Treaty Organization, *Wales Summit Declaration* (Sept. 5, 2014), available online at <http://www.nato.int/cps/en/natohq/official_texts_112964.htm#cyber> ("To face this evolving challenge, we have endorsed an Enhanced Cyber Defence Policy, contributing to the fulfillment of the Alliance's core tasks. The policy reaffirms the principles of the indivisibility of Allied security and of prevention, detection, resilience, recovery, and defence…. Cyber attacks can reach a threshold that threatens national and Euro-Atlantic prosperity, security, and stability. Their impact could be as harmful to modern societies as a conventional attack. We affirm therefore that cyber defence is part of NATO's core task of collective defence. A decision as to when a cyber attack would lead to the invocation of Article 5 would be taken by the North Atlantic Council on a case-by-case basis.").

self-defense does not require a nation to actually wait until an actual armed attack takes place and the consequences are suffered, in order to invoke its right of self-defense against an imminent, pressing threat.[12] Moreover, the decision of whether or not to go to war, what constitutes a just cause for war, and how a nation chooses to respond, including the means of warfare it uses in response, are profoundly moral questions with implications for the overall conduct of such conflicts going forward and the ethical constraints we can, and should, apply to ourselves in conducting even a war that is just and legal. These are issues that must be debated, both here at home, as well as through international institutions, so that we can at least see if it is possible to develop the beginnings of a reasonable international consensus on these matters.

In looking at these questions, particularly in a new domain like cyberspace, we have to think not just about the right and left boundaries of what constitutes acts of war and how and when we might respond, but also about the vital center, and the hard questions that lie within. And while there are no detailed answers to be immediately had in short form, we are also not writing on a blank slate: many have considered the implications on just war theory and international law of new domains or new methods or warfare before, whether with the advent of air war or the development (and use) of nuclear weapons.[13] Perhaps even more importantly, we are not even writing on a blank slate when it comes to cyberspace in particular. The Tallinn Manual, a NATO-sponsored effort, provides helpful guidance in this area,[14] and will likely continue to do so, as it is currently in the process of being updated.

When it comes to determining, whether as a legal, political, and moral/ethical matter, what type of acts constitute an act of war, there are some basic constructs one can look towards. First, it seems obvious that the extent of and nature of the damage caused will have some impact on this decision. Second, the intent of the threat actor matters. The nature and type of the systems or data affected by the attack will also certainly play a role, as will the potential immediate and downstream impact of the attack, including the economic, political, and social aspects of such impact. And, perhaps even more importantly, the ability to identify the source of the attack and publicly attribute it may play a crucial role in determining whether a given attack constitutes an act of war and whether or how a given nation might respond. It is fairly obvious

---

[12] *See, e.g.*, White House, *The National Security Strategy of the United States of America* (Sept. 2002), *available online at* <http://www.state.gov/documents/organization/63562.pdf> ("For centuries, international law recognized that nations need not suffer an attack before they can lawfully take action to defend themselves against forces that present an imminent danger of attack. Legal scholars and international jurists often conditioned the legitimacy of preemption on the existence of an imminent threat—most often a visible mobilization of armies, navies, and air forces preparing to attack."); Brian Egan, *International Law, Legal Diplomacy, and the Counter-ISIL Campaign* (Apr. 4, 2016), *available online at* <https://www.justsecurity.org/wp-content/uploads/2016/04/Egan-ASIL-speech.pdf> ("Under the jus ad bellum, a State may use force in the exercise of its inherent right of self-defense not only in response to armed attacks that have occurred, but also in response to imminent ones before they occur....The absence of specific evidence of where an attack will take place or of the precise nature of an attack does not preclude a conclusion that an armed attack is imminent for purposes of the exercise of the right of self-defense, provided that there is a reasonable and objective basis for concluding that an armed attack is imminent.")

[13] *See, e.g.*, W. Hays Parks, *Air War and the Law of War*, 32 A.F. L. Rev. 1 (1990); Jill M. Sheldon, *Note: Nuclear Weapons and the Laws of War: Does Customary International Law Prohibit the use of Nuclear Weapons in all Circumstances?*, 20 Fordham Int'l L.J. 181 (1996) (collecting materials).

[14] *See* NATO Cooperative Cyber Defence Centre of Excellence, *Tallinn Manual on the International Law Applicable to Cyber Warfare* (2013), *available online at* <https://ccdcoe.org/tallinn-manual.html>.

where an attack is coming from if you see a land-based missile launched with a particular radar or heat signature or a bomber flying over your territory; it is much harder when the attacker is coming at you in cyberspace across a series of hop-points, some of which may be in your own territory, and employing sophisticated obfuscation methods that are widely accessible to a broad range of actors.

Beyond determining whether an act of war has actually taken place, one must be prepared to consider what might be done in response to such an act. Today as it stands, there is very little talk about our cyber capabilities, whether it comes to offense or defense. While it is not obvious that an attack in cyberspace requires a response in the same domain, it is fair to assume that a cyber response must at least be part of the calculus. Without much public discussion of our basic cyber capabilities, particularly on offense, we face two major challenges: it is difficult to have a reasoned discussion of how we might respond—at least in the cyber domain—and it is that much harder to deter offensive actions by others. After all, basic deterrence theory is premised on the notion of being clear on what a nation would likely to do in response to a defined set of actions by an attacker. Without talking about capabilities and defining what set of actions would trigger the use of those capabilities (as well as a clear willingness to actually undertake such a response), it is no surprise that deterrence does not work particularly well today in the cyber domain. And this is all the more important as we see the spread of cyber capabilities to more unpredictable nation-state actors, as discussed above, and even more worryingly, perhaps in the longer-run, to non-state, asymmetric actors like terrorist groups.

The fact of the matter is that today we are not well equipped to address these threats. We have yet to fully think through the doctrine or strategies in this area, much less the authorities and the rules of engagement. And while U.S. Cyber Command is beginning to build the forces and capabilities necessary to carry out this mission on behalf of the U.S. government and our nation, we are a long way from getting to where we need to be to make sure we do it right. In doing so, we also need to make sure that the Department of Defense and the Intelligence Community are properly postured to protect the nation, both through the collection of intelligence and the readiness to respond. This means, in part, that the current approach to ensuring full cooperation and coordination through the dual-hatting of the Director of NSA and Commander of U.S. Cyber Command ought not be undermined by nascent efforts to divide the two out of a need for improved optics. Undermining our readiness and capability to act swiftly in order to address perception issues sets us on exactly the wrong course.

The current situation is particularly troubling because the reality is that the enemy will not wait for us to get this right. We cannot rely on a false sense of security; while our systems today are fairly resilient and we are working harder to make them more so, we must do more. Perhaps most importantly, given the fact that the vast majority of our key networked infrastructure is owned and operated by the private sector, the government and the private sector must learn to work together to defend our nation in cyberspace. Assuming that either the private sector or the government standing alone will be able to defend our nation is tantamount to the French reliance on the Maginot Line during the lead-up to World War II. We ought not repeat that historically catastrophic mistake.

I'm glad to be here today to discuss these issues with you and look forward to answering your questions.

Mr. HURD. Thank you, General Alexander.

Now it's always a pleasure to introduce my friend and colleague from the great State of Illinois, Ms. Robin Kelly, the ranking member of the Subcommittee on IT.

Ms. KELLY. Thank you, my friend.

I'd like to thank Chairman Hurd and Chairman DeSantis for calling this hearing so that the committee and the American people can get a better understanding of when a cyber attack should be considered an at act of war and how the United States might respond when that happens.

The cyber threats facing the United States are increasing in severity, opening the Nation to the possibility of extremely damaging cyber strikes that could potentially threaten the U.S. Economy and endanger American lives.

General Alexander, in your 2014 testimony before the Senate Committee on Armed Services you warned, and I quote, "Those attacks are coming, and I think those are near term, and we're not ready for them."

In fact, we are already seeing the first salvos of digital attack reaching beyond the cyber realm. In March of this year, seven members of Iran's Revolutionary Guard Corps hacked into the control system of the Bowman Avenue Dam in Rye Brook, New York. In response to the compromise of the dam's cyber network, Paul Rosenberg, the mayor said, and I quote, "It's ridiculous how little that dam is, how insignificant in the grand scheme of things. We're not talking about something vital to the infrastructure of the country."

While May's attack may not have targeted the Nation's vital critical infrastructure, it's almost certain that future attacks will, and when that does happen, how do we react? Do we hack the hackers, or do we respond with physical force? This isn't the first time Congress and the intelligence community have tried to answer that question.

It is important that we recognize that the global nature of the Internet requires the U.S. to establish solid partnerships throughout the international community so that every nation understands that there are consequences for unacceptable cyber behavior. The problem is that by laying out in a public forum what constitutes unacceptable, we open the possibility that our adversaries know where the tripwires lie across which they can't step.

That's why I'm pleased the chairman has arranged for committee members to receive a classified briefing to better understand where that line is and how we respond when our enemies cross that line.

And again, I'd like to thank the chairman for calling this hearing and our witnesses for being here today.

Mr. HURD. Thank you, Ms. Kelly.

Now we'll go to Mr. Hughes for your 5 minutes of opening statements.

STATEMENT OF AARON HUGHES

Mr. HUGHES. Thank you, Chairmen Hurd and DeSantis, Ranking Members Kelly and Lynch, and members of the subcommittees. I'm pleased to testify today on the Department of Defense's strategy as it relates to cyberspace and how the Department approaches cyber incidents. It is an honor to be here, and I'm proud of the progress we have made in this challenging domain.

Since DOD's Cyber Strategy was signed in April of 2015, the Department has devoted considerable resources to implementing the goals and objectives outlined within the document. When Secretary Carter signed the Strategy, he directed the Department to focus its efforts on three primary missions in cyberspace. First, to defend DOD networks, systems, and information to assure DOD missions. Second, to defend the United States against cyber attacks of significant consequence. And to provide integrated cyber capabilities in support of military operations and contingency plans

Another key aspect of our strategy is deterrence. DOD is supporting a comprehensive whole-of-government cyber deterrence strategy to defer attacks on U.S. interests. This strategy depends on the totality of U.S. actions, to include declaratory policy, overall defensive posture, effective response options, indications and warning capabilities, and the resilience of U.S. networks and systems.

That said, incidents described as cyber attacks or computer network attacks are not necessarily armed attacks for the purposes of triggering a nation-state's inherent right of self-defense. When determining whether a cyber incident constitutes an armed attack, the U.S. Government considers a broad range of factors, including the nature and extent of injury or death to persons and the destruction of or damage to property. As such, cyber incidents are assessed on a case-by-case basis, and we would use a whole-of-government approach in responding to and deterring future malicious activities in cyberspace.

The fact of the matter is that we face diverse and persistent threats in cyberspace from state and nonstate actors that cannot be defeated through the efforts of any single organization. Our increasingly wired and interconnected world has brought prosperity and economic gain to the United States, while our dependence on these systems has left us vulnerable to the evolving threats posed by malicious cyber activity.

While DOD maintains and uses robust and unique cyber capabilities to defend our networks and the Nation, that alone is not sufficient. Securing our systems and networks is everyone's responsibility and requires close collaboration with other Federal departments, our allies and partners internationally, and the private sector to improve our Nation's cybersecurity posture and to ensure that DOD has the ability to operate in any environment at any time.

The Department is committed to enhancing the resilience of our networks and systems and defending the U.S. homeland and U.S. interests from attacks of significant consequence that may occur in cyberspace. I look forward to working with these committees and the Congress to ensure that DOD has the necessary capabilities to carry out our roles and missions in cyberspace and to keep our country safe. I thank you for the support in these efforts, and I look forward to your questions this afternoon.

Thank you.

[Prepared statement of Mr. Hughes follows:]

INTRODUCTION

Chairmen Hurd and DeSantis, Ranking Members Kelly and Lynch, and Members of the Subcommittees, thank you for inviting me to discuss the Department of Defense's (DoD) strategy as it relates to cyberspace and how that applies to cyberattacks. It is an honor to appear before you today, and I appreciate the opportunity to explain the progress the Department is making to improve America's cybersecurity posture.

I plan to focus my testimony on the Department's strategy and missions in cyberspace, including through deterrence, and the threats and challenges posed by State and non-state actors. Improving our collective cyber defenses is a whole-of-government and whole-of-nation endeavor that also requires close cooperation with our allies, partners, and the private sector.

DOD STRATEGY AND MISSIONS

Recognizing that DoD relies heavily on cyberspace for virtually everything we do, the Department's Cyber Strategy guides our efforts in cyberspace. The Strategy directs the Department to focus its efforts on three primary missions in cyberspace: (1) defend DoD information networks to ensure DoD mission effectiveness, (2) defend the United States against cyberattacks of significant consequence, and (3) provide full-spectrum cyber options to support contingency plans and military operations.

One of the Department's key policy goals in cyberspace is to deter cyberattacks. Incidents described as "cyberattacks" or "computer network attacks" are not necessarily "armed attacks" for the purposes of triggering a nation-state's inherent right of self-defense (as recognized in Article 51 of the United Nations Charter). In that vein, when determining whether a cyber incident constitutes an armed attack, the U.S. Government considers a number of factors including the nature and extent of injury or death to persons and the destruction of, or damage to, property. As such, cyber incidents are assessed on a case-by-case basis and, as the President has publicly stated, the U.S. Government's response to any particular cyber incident would come "in a place and time and manner that we choose."

DoD is supporting a comprehensive, whole-of-government cyber deterrence strategy to deter cyberattacks against U.S. interests. This strategy depends on the totality of U.S. actions, including its declaratory policy, overall defensive posture, effective response procedures, indications and warning capabilities, and the resiliency of U.S. networks and systems.

Fundamentally, deterrence is largely a function of perception, and DoD has three specific roles to play within a whole-of-government deterrence strategy. First, we seek to deny the adversary the ability to achieve the objectives of a cyberattack, so our adversary will believe any attack will be futile. We do this through strengthening our cyber defenses and reducing our attack surface. Second, we want to improve our resilience so our adversary will perceive that, even if any single attack is successful, we can reconstitute quickly so that their ultimate objective will not be achieved. The Department is already training to operate in a "cyber contested environment," to demonstrate that we can continue our mission even while under cyberattack. Lastly, for deterrence to be effective, the adversaries must believe that our ability to respond to an attack will result in unacceptable costs imposed on them. Costs may be imposed through a variety of mechanisms, including economic sanctions, diplomacy, law enforcement, and military action. Our task at the Department is to plan and prepare to conduct military operations, including through cyberspace, to impose costs on the adversary.

THE CYBER LANDSCAPE

We continue to face a diverse and persistent set of threats from State and non-state actors who probe and scan DoD networks for vulnerabilities. Although the United States has benefited greatly from the increasingly wired and interconnected global landscape, cyber threats are evolving, posing greater risks to the networks and systems of the Department of Defense and other Federal departments and agencies, our national critical infrastructure, and U.S. companies and interests.

In the last few years, there have been numerous high-profile malicious cyber or cyber-enabled events that have captured the public's attention, including incidents that have affected Sony Pictures Entertainment, the U.S. Office of Personnel Management (OPM), the Department of Defense unclassified Joint Staff network, and the Ukrainian power grid. If malicious cyber actors gain access to DoD networks, they can potentially manipulate information or software, destroy data, and impair the functioning of systems that computers control. Although DoD maintains and uses robust and unique cyber capabilities to defend our networks, often these measures alone are not sufficient. Securing systems and networks is everyone's responsibility – from the commander down to the individual network user and across the Federal Government – and requires a culture of cybersecurity.

Criminal activity in cyberspace is a significant and growing problem, but nations in many ways still represent the gravest threats because of the skill and resources they can bring to bear. The States that we watch most closely in cyberspace remain Russia, China, Iran, and North Korea. Russia and China have developed advanced cyber capabilities and strategies, and Russian actors in particular are stealthy in their cyber tradecraft, and their intentions are sometimes difficult to discern. In September 2015, the U.S. and China agreed to neither conduct nor knowingly support the cyber-enabled theft of intellectual property for commercial gain; we continue to monitor China's compliance. Iran and North Korea have demonstrated the capability and willingness to conduct damaging and destructive cyber-attacks against the United States in support of their policy objectives. Finally, the Islamic State of Iraq and the Levant (ISIL) represents a serious and complex threat, and continues to use the Internet to intimidate its enemies, recruit fighters, incite violence, and inspire attacks. As part of the efforts of the 66-member Global Coalition to counter ISIL, the Department is providing integrated cyber capabilities and support to Operation INHERENT RESOLVE.

At DoD, protecting the territory and people of the United States remains our highest priority, and we remain vigilant, and devote substantial resources and effort preparing for threats that could be directed against the U.S. homeland, and infrastructure that the Department relies on to operate during a contingency.

INTERNATIONAL COOPERATION

In line with the President's 2011 *United States International Strategy for Cyberspace*, the Department works with foreign partners bilaterally and multilaterally – through NATO, for example – to advance cyberspace cooperation to defend U.S., allied, and partner interests. Our international partners bring varying capabilities and expertise, but the Department prioritizes international cyberspace partnerships to enhance cyber defense and to build greater collective security. Cooperation in cyberspace increases our capacity to detect, monitor, prevent, and defeat threats in cyberspace while working to ensure that our allies and international partners develop and build strong cyber defense capabilities.

Beyond the Department's engagements with the international community, DoD supports the Department of State's diplomatic efforts to promote a framework for stability in cyberspace that includes affirmation of the applicability of international law to state conduct in cyberspace, the identification of voluntary peacetime norms of state behavior in cyberspace, and the promotion of cyber confidence-building measures. In particular, as voluntary measures of self-restraint, the Department believes peacetime norms can contribute to conflict prevention and stability.

CONCLUSION

The Department is committed to the security and resiliency of our networks and to defending the U.S. homeland and interests from cyberattacks of significant consequence. We have undertaken comprehensive efforts, both unilaterally and in concert with our allies and partners, and the private sector to improve our Nation's cybersecurity posture and to ensure that DoD has the ability to operate in any environment at any time. Our relationship with Congress is absolutely critical to everything the Department is doing in cyberspace. To that end, I am grateful for the Committee's interest in these issues, and I look forward to your questions.

Mr. HURD. Thank you, Mr. Hughes.

Mr. Painter, you're now recognized for 5 minutes.

STATEMENT OF CHRIS PAINTER

Mr. PAINTER. Chairmen Hurd and DeSantis, Ranking Members Kelly and Lynch, members of the Subcommittees for Information Technology and National Security, thank you for the opportunity to speak to you today. I will discuss the framework for stability in cyberspace at the State Department, in particular it's working to promote internationally, but with our partners. I will also cover some of the other topics that were raised in your invitation.

The Department of State, working with our interagency partners, is guided by the President's 2011 International Strategy for Cyberspace, which sets out a strategic framework of international cyber stability designed to achieve and maintain a peaceful cyberspace environment where all states are able to fully realize its benefits, where there are advantages to cooperating against common threats and avoiding conflict, and where there is little incentive for states to engage in disruptive behavior or to attack one another.

This framework has three key elements. First, the affirmation that existing international law applies to state behavior in cyberspace. Second, the development of an international consensus on and promotion of additional voluntary norms of responsible state behavior in cyberspace that apply during peacetime. And third, the development and implementation of practical confidence-building measures, or CBMs, among states.

Although many of the elements of this framework may seem self-evident to a U.S. audience, especially a sophisticated one, cyber issues are still new to many states, and there are also states that hold alternative views of how to promote cyber stability. Notwithstanding these headwinds, as well as the fact that diplomatic negotiations on other issues can take many years, if not decades, the United States and its partners have made substantial and really big progress in recent years toward advancing our strategic framework for international cyber stability.

Since 2009, the United Nations Group of Governmental Experts on International Security Issues in Cyberspace, or the UN GGE, has served as a productive and groundbreaking expert-level venue for the United States to build support for this framework through three consensus reports in 2010, 2013, and 2015. I should emphasize the U.S. has been the leader here. The conclusions captured in those reports have in turn been endorsed by political leaders in a range of settings, including most recently at the G–20 leaders summit in Turkey.

Given the title of this hearing, "Digital Acts of War," I would like to discuss how the U.S. Government thinks about these issues, which is consistent with its broader approach to promoting stability in cyberspace through the prism of existing international law

As an initial matter, the United States has been clear that it believes that cyber activities may, in certain circumstances, constitute an armed attack that triggers our inherent right to self-defense as recognized by Article 51 of the U.N. Charter. The United States has described publicly how it will evaluate whether a cyber activity constitutes an armed attack under international law. Of primary importance to such a determination are the actual or anticipated effects of a particular incident.

When determining whether a cyber activity constitutes an armed attack sufficient to trigger a state's inherent right to self-defense, the U.S. Government believes a state should consider the nature and extent of the injury or death to persons and the destruction of or damage to property, an effects-based test.

It is worth emphasizing that this is a case-by-case, fact-specific inquiry, whether the events in question occur in cyberspace or elsewhere. As a general matter, states have not sought to define precisely or state conclusively what situations would constitute armed attacks in other domains, and there is no reason cyberspace should be different. In fact, strategic ambiguity could very well deter most states from getting close to the threshold of an armed attack.

Finally, I would hasten to note that regardless of whether a particular incident rises to the level of an armed attack, we have a range of options for responding. The U.S. Government uses a whole-of-government approach to responding to and deterring malicious activities in cyberspace that brings to bear its full range of instruments of national power and corresponding policy tools—diplomatic, law enforcement, economic, military, and intelligence—as appropriate and consistent with applicable law in particular cases.

As suggested in the invitation for this hearing, public attribution is one such option. In cases where actors responsible for a particular incident have been determined, the U.S. Government will consider whether to identify those actors publicly when we believe it will further our national interest, including our ability to hold those actors accountable. However, the U.S. Government will also maintain flexibility to avail itself of the full suite of options that we have.

In closing, I would like to thank the two subcommittees for giving me an opportunity to speak on such a relevant and timely set of issues. Despite the threats we face in cyberspace, I know that we are all committed to maintaining and promoting an open, interoperable, secure, and reliable Internet in the face of these threats that we can all continue to benefit from.

On a personal note, I've been involved in these issues, as the chairman has mentioned, for the last 24 years now, almost 25, and I'm very pleased to see that they are getting the attention as a policy priority both within the U.S. and around the world, and I certainly think we've made a lot progress in having the kind of conversation that was discussed earlier. And I look forward to your questions.

[Prepared statement of Mr. Painter follows:]

Testimony of Christopher M. E. Painter, Coordinator for Cyber Issues
U.S. Department of State
Before the House of Representatives Committee on Oversight and Government Reform
Subcommittees on Information Security and National Security

Hearing on "Digital Acts of War: Evolving the Cybersecurity Conversation"

July 13, 2016

Chairmen Hurd and DeSantis, Ranking Members Kelly and Lynch, members of the Subcommittee on Information Technology and the Subcommittee on National Security, thank you for the opportunity to speak to you today on this very timely subject.

Over the last few decades, the Internet and information and communications technologies (ICTs) more broadly have brought profound benefits to the United States and the rest of the world – enabling innovation, connecting people to information and services, and providing a new forum for people to express their views and to dissent. Given all of these benefits as well as our growing dependence on technology, it is not surprising that governments as well as certain non-state actors have increasingly come to view cyberspace as a place where they too can pursue their objectives. A number of militaries around the world – including our own – have publicly stated their intention to operate in cyberspace, while still more are actively developing their cyber capabilities. Reports of cyber incidents potentially linked to state-sponsored activity have become a regular feature of the public conversation on cybersecurity issues.

Although there is no question that we face new challenges, our goal remains what was articulated in the President's 2011 U.S. *International Strategy for Cyberspace*: "to promote an open, interoperable, secure, and reliable information and communications infrastructure that supports international trade and commerce, strengthens international security, and fosters free expression and innovation." We must work every day to ensure that even as the number and variety of online threats grow and evolve, the Internet remains a place where people can do business, connect with friends, and express their views. We need to ensure that the Internet remains a greater source of stability than it is a source of instability and that governments and other actors behave responsibly as they conduct their activities in cyberspace. In short, we need a framework for international stability in cyberspace.

During my time today, I will discuss the framework for stability in cyberspace that the U.S. government and the State Department in particular are working to promote internationally and some of our recent successes in that regard. Much of what I will address on this topic is also covered by the *Department of State International Cyberspace Policy Strategy* that was submitted in April as required by the Consolidated Appropriations Act for 2016 (Public Law 114-113). I will also discuss some of the other topics raised in your invitation, including when an incident in cyberspace might rise to level of an armed attack and how the U.S. government thinks about the proper response to individual cyber incidents, including through public attribution.

Building a Framework for International Stability in Cyberspace

The Department of State, working with our interagency partners, is guided by the vision of the President's *International Strategy for Cyberspace*, which is to promote a strategic framework of international cyber stability designed to achieve and maintain a peaceful cyberspace environment where all states are able to fully realize its benefits, where there are advantages to cooperating against common threats and avoiding conflict, and where there is little incentive for states to engage in disruptive behavior or to attack one another.

This framework has three key elements: (1) global affirmation that international law applies to state behavior in cyberspace; (2) development of an international consensus on and promotion of additional voluntary norms of responsible state behavior in cyberspace that apply during peacetime; and (3) development and implementation of practical confidence-building measures (CBMs) among states, which promote stability in cyberspace by reducing the risks of misperception and escalation.

Since 2009, the United Nations Group of Governmental Experts on Developments in the Field of Information and Telecommunications in the Context of International Security (UN GGE) has served as a productive and groundbreaking expert-level venue for the United States to build support for this framework. The consensus recommendations of the three UN GGE reports in 2010, 2013, and 2015 have set the standard for the international community on the applicability of international law in cyberspace, voluntary peacetime norms, and CBMs. The conclusions captured in these reports have in turn been endorsed by political leaders in a range of settings. When it reconvenes in August 2016, the UN GGE process will continue to play a central role in our efforts to promulgate this framework fully.

<u>Applicability of international law</u>. The first and most fundamental pillar of our framework for international cyber stability is the applicability of existing international law to state behavior in cyberspace. The 2013 UN GGE report was a significant achievement that affirmed the applicability of existing international law, including the UN Charter, to state conduct in cyberspace. The 2013 report underscored that states must act in cyberspace under the established international obligations and commitments that have guided their actions for decades – in peacetime and during conflict – and that states must meet their international obligations regarding internationally wrongful acts attributable to them. The 2014-2015 UN GGE also made progress on issues related to international law by highlighting that the UN Charter applies in its entirety, affirming the applicability of the inherent right of self-defense as recognized in Article 51 of the UN Charter, and noting the law of armed conflict's fundamental principles of humanity, necessity, proportionality, and distinction.

<u>Norms of responsible state behavior</u>. The United States is also building consensus on a set of additional, voluntary norms of responsible state behavior in cyberspace that define key areas of risk that would be of national and/or economic security concern to all states and that should be off-limits during times of peace. If observed, these stability measures – which are measures of self-restraint – can contribute substantially to conflict prevention and stability. The United States was the first state to propose a set of specific peacetime cyber norms. Those norms are as follows:

- A state should not conduct or knowingly support online activity that intentionally damages critical infrastructure or otherwise impairs the use of critical infrastructure to provide services to the public.

- A state should not conduct or knowingly support activity intended to prevent national computer security incident response teams (CSIRTs) from responding to cyber incidents. A State should also not use CSIRTs to enable online activity that is intended to do harm.

- A state should cooperate, in a manner consistent with its domestic law and international obligations, with requests for assistance from other states in investigating cybercrimes, collecting electronic evidence, and mitigating malicious cyber activity emanating from its territory.

- A state should not conduct or knowingly support cyber-enabled theft of intellectual property, including trade secrets or other confidential business information, with the intent of providing competitive advantages to its companies or commercial sectors.

In May 2015, Secretary of State Kerry highlighted these norms in his speech in Seoul, South Korea, on an open and secure Internet. The 2015 UN GGE report's most significant achievement was its recommendation for voluntary norms of state behavior designed for peacetime, which included concepts championed by the United States.

Confidence-building measures. Together with our work on international law and voluntary norms, cyber CBMs have the potential to contribute substantially to international cyber stability. CBMs have been used by governments for decades to build confidence, reduce risk, and increase transparency in other areas of international concern. Examples of cyber CBMs include: transparency measures, such as sharing national strategies or doctrine; cooperative measures, such as building points of contact networks to respond rapidly to cyber incidents; and stability measures, such as committing to refrain from a certain activity of concern. Cyber CBMs are being developed, and are in the first stages of implementation, in two regional venues – the Organization for Security and Cooperation in Europe (OSCE) and the ASEAN Regional Forum where agreement was reached in 2015 on a detailed work plan with a proposed set of CBMs for future implementation.

Although many of the elements of the framework I have described above may seem self-evident to a U.S. audience, it is important to recognize that cyber issues are new to many states and, as I am happy to discuss during the question and answer period, there are also states that hold alternative views on how to promote cyber stability. Notwithstanding these headwinds, as well as the fact that diplomatic negotiations on other issues can take many years, if not decades, the United States and its allies and partners have made substantial progress in recent years towards advancing our strategic framework of international cyber stability.

In addition to the GGE reports, I would like to briefly highlight a few examples from the last year that reflect our progress in achieving broader adoption of the framework.

- First, in September 2015, during President Xi Jinping's state visit, the United States and China made several key commitments on cyber issues. These include a commitment that neither country's government will conduct or knowingly support cyber-enabled theft of intellectual property for commercial advantage, as well as a statement welcoming the 2015 GGE report.

- Second, last November, the leaders of the G20, meeting in Antalya, Turkey, strongly endorsed the U.S. approach to promoting stability in cyberspace. The leaders' communique affirmed that states should not conduct or support the cyber-enabled theft of intellectual property for commercial advantage. The communique also highlighted the 2015 UN GGE report I discussed; affirmed that international law, and in particular the UN Charter, applies to state conduct in cyberspace; and endorsed the view that all states should abide by norms of responsible state behavior in cyberspace.

- Finally, although it received less publicity than the previous two developments, the 57 member states of the OSCE, which includes not only the United States and its Western allies and partners but also Russia and other former Soviet states, reached consensus in March 2016 on an expanded set of CBMs. This expanded set, which includes five new cooperative CBMs, focusing on issues like cybersecurity of critical infrastructure and developing public-private partnerships as well as mechanisms for the exchange of best practices, builds upon the existing 11 CBMs announced in 2013 that focus on building transparency and putting in place mechanisms for de-escalating conflict.

On the Concept of a "Digital Act of War"

Given the title of this hearing, "Digital Acts of War," I would like to discuss how the U.S. government thinks about these issues, which, consistent with its broader approach to promoting stability in cyberspace, is through the prism of existing international law.

As an initial matter, the United States has been clear that it believes that cyber activities may in certain circumstances constitute an armed attack that triggers our inherent right of self-defense, as recognized in Article 51 of the UN Charter.

The United States has described publicly how it would evaluate whether a cyber activity constitutes an armed attack under international law. Of primary importance to such a determination are the actual or anticipated effects of a particular incident. When determining whether a cyber activity constitutes an armed attack sufficient to trigger a state's inherent right of self-defense, the U.S. government believes that states should consider the nature and extent of injury or death to persons and the destruction of, or damage to, property. Although this is necessarily a case-by-case, fact-specific inquiry, in general, cyber activities that proximately result in death, injury, or significant destruction, or represent an imminent threat thereof, likely would be viewed as an armed attack.

It is worth emphasizing that a determination whether specific events constitute an actual or imminent armed attack sufficient to trigger a state's inherent right of self-defense is necessarily a case-by-case, fact-specific inquiry. This is the case whether the events occur in cyberspace or elsewhere. As a general matter, states have not sought to define precisely (or state conclusively) what situations would constitute armed attacks in other domains, and there is no reason cyberspace should be different. In fact, there is a good reason not to articulate a bright line, as strategic ambiguity could very well deter most states from getting close to it.

Responding to Cyber Incidents

Finally, I would hasten to note that the U.S. government uses a whole-of-government approach to responding to and deterring malicious activities in cyberspace. This approach brings to bear its full range of instruments of national power and corresponding policy tools – diplomatic, law enforcement, economic, military, and intelligence – as appropriate and consistent with applicable law. This means that regardless of whether a particular incident rises to the level of an armed attack, the President has a range of options for responding.

As suggested in the invitation for this hearing, public attribution is one such option. In cases where the actors responsible for a particular incident have been determined, the U.S. government will consider whether to identify those actors publicly when we believe it will further our national interests, including our ability to hold the actors accountable. North Korea's 2014 cyber attack against Sony Pictures Entertainment, for example, which rendered thousands of computers inoperable and was intended to interfere with the exercise of freedom of expression and inflict significant harm on a U.S. business, represented behavior in cyberspace that is simply unacceptable. This, in combination with the strength of the evidence linking North Korea to the cyber attack, contributed to the U.S. government's decision to make a public attribution in that case. However, the U.S. government also maintains the flexibility to avail itself of the other options that I have mentioned as appropriate.

* * *

In closing, I would like to express my appreciation for both Subcommittees' interest in these important topics. I look forward to addressing your questions.

Mr. HURD. Thank you, Mr. Painter.

Mr. Kanuck, you're now recognized for 5 minutes.

STATEMENT OF SEAN KANUCK

Mr. KANUCK. Thank you very much, Chairman Hurd, Chairman DeSantis, Ranking Member Lynch, Ranking Member Kelly, and distinguished members of Congress. It is indeed a pleasure to be here and contribute to this important discussion.

Having looked at it as an academic, as a professional international attorney, and as a national intelligence officer for 5 years until last May, I come with a genuinely strategic and analytic approach. I have not been involved in policy formulation directly in the past. And I concur with my colleagues about the importance of this topic, and after 15, 20 years of my own experience, I, too, am excited to see the public and congressional attention being paid to this important issue.

I will offer, however, that as a Nation we still lack both a strategic approach to this problem and a practical, effective set of solutions to deter malicious and adversarial behavior in cyberspace, and that itself is illustrated by the myriad cyber attacks we read about each year that are perpetrated by a range of state and nonstate actors.

In my written testimony, I address several of the questions that my colleagues have also mentioned, so let me very briefly say that I concur with Mr. Hughes and Mr. Painter that digital acts of war will be judged through an effects-based analysis. In my academic work since 1996, I've held that position, and I do agree with the U.S. Government representatives here today that that is the correct approach.

Regarding the issue of attribution challenges, I will note, in my analytic work for the intelligence community we looked at two considerations. We looked at the technical or forensic aspects—network investigations, malicious software, reverse engineering, and other digital footprints—in addition to what I term analytic attribution, where you looked at the geopolitical context within which malicious cyber events happen.

In many cases, the context, the identity of the target, and how the information that was stolen, compromised, or made unavailable is used or leveraged can oftentimes tell you about the motivation and possibly the actor. That's from the analytic and technical attribution side.

A completely distinct question is whether or not one would seek to do public attribution, and that is inherently a policy question for policymakers. It has three components, in my opinion.

There's the question about the bilateral relationship with any entity you may accuse of an action. Cyber does not occur in its own stovepipe or domain. It's a part of much larger international and bilateral relationships.

Secondly, the decision of whether or not to compromise sources and methods of intelligence in order to prove, evidentiary, why that attribution assessment is being offered publicly. Obviously, there would be policy reasons to not disclose certain intelligence capabilities, especially in a context where those capabilities may be perishable and they may be the exact same platforms or accesses that one may use for a retaliatory capability.

So it's almost a double negative potential if you choose to publicly attribute in that context because you don't have separate reconnaissance platforms in all cases and separate retaliatory platforms the way you would have had in a nuclear context, for example.

Last of all, as I believe Ranking Member Kelly may have mentioned, the issue of credible threats and credible deterrents. If you are not prepared or capable of exacting satisfaction upon accusing or attributing an action to someone, what does that do for your global reputation and the import of any of your declaratory statements?

Those three very important policy questions are very distinct from the technical attribution questions, but equally important from a policy perspective.

I will also commend the U.S. diplomats who have had what I think are great successes in the U.N. Group of Governmental Experts, the G–20, OSCE, and with particularly President Xi and the People's Republic of China. However, I am not personally convinced that diplomatic overtures directly translate into changes of behavior, particularly when Western countries like the United States continue to have fundamentally different objectives for international cybersecurity than certain other nations, such as Russia and China, and my written statement addresses some of that basal difference.

I will also offer that I see a de facto norm today, which is: Do cyber operations, do them clandestinely, and try to get away with them, you might not be punished. And, in fact, Director Clapper's testimony in 2016 read, "Many actors remain undeterred from conducting reconnaissance, espionage, and even attacks in cyberspace because of the relatively low cost of entry, the perceived payoff, and the lack of significant consequences."

My time has concluded, so I will leave that there for now. Thank you very much. And once again, thank for the invitation to participate.

[Prepared statement of Mr. Kanuck follows:]

Chairman Hurd, Chairman DeSantis, Ranking Member Kelly, Ranking Member Lynch, and distinguished Members of Congress:

It is my honor and privilege to participate in the hearing entitled "Digital Acts of War: Evolving the Cybersecurity Conversation" before the Subcommittees on Information Technology and National Security of the Committee on Oversight and Government Reform of the House of Representatives. I thank you for your invitation and sincerely hope that my contribution will assist you in your work on this critical topic.

This Statement for the Record draws upon my twenty years of experience in the field of information and communication technologies (ICT), including: as an academic, as a professional attorney who specializes in public international law, and as a senior intelligence officer for the United States Government. The perspective offered herein has been ineluctably shaped by my service as the National Intelligence Officer for Cyber Issues (NIO/Cyber) from May 2011 to May 2016. Having led strategic cyber analysis for the US Intelligence Community for five years, I earnestly concur in the need to evolve the cyber security conversation beyond where it is today. That will require (1) deeper subject matter expertise by more policy makers and legislators, (2) broader inclusion of private sector concerns and recommendations in public policy, and (3) a genuinely strategic approach that is currently lacking.

Since 2013, the Director of National Intelligence has led his annual, written Worldwide Threat Assessment to Congress with the cyber topic because ICT not only pose a cyber security risk in their own right, but also are integral factors utilized in the conduct of nearly every national security threat today.[1] During my tenure as NIO/Cyber, the US Intelligence Community attempted to provide policy makers with a strategic framework to understand cyber threats and strove to dispel several misnomers about cyberspace, namely: (a) it is not a unique physical "domain"; (b) it does not fulfill the logical criteria of a "global commons"; (c) not all adversarial cyber operations qualify as "attacks"; and (d) a "cyber Armageddon" is a highly improbable scenario. Rather than revisiting those questions that have been previously addressed elsewhere, this Statement will simply take those understandings as its point of departure.[2]

In order to evolve the cyber security conversation, one must first know what has or has not already been established and/or achieved. For example, the question of what constitutes a digital act of war has been studied for over twenty years. Rigorous legal scholarship by both myself and Michael Schmitt in the mid-to-late 1990s concluded that an effects-based analysis would be required to assess the applicability of Articles 2(4) and 51 of the United Nations Charter.[3] Most academic commentators around the world who subsequently turned to that same question have arrived at a similar conclusion. The extreme difficulty of observing or detecting actions in cyberspace – let alone divining intentions – leaves one with effects as the only legitimate measure upon which to base policy responses. The academic, non-binding Tallinn Manual (for which Michael Schmitt has served as editor) perhaps now offers the strongest and most articulate exegesis of the effects-based doctrine.[4] It essentially says that what constitutes an act of war is largely agnostic of the modality used to perpetrate the harm(s). Accordingly, a special notion of a "digital" act of war is yet another misnomer.

Politicians and the media may try to label significant espionage successes or compromises of personally identifiable information (PII) as acts of cyber war, but such parlance does not comport with legal reasoning. That does not mean that a wide array of policy options – ranging from demarches to sanctions to domestic law enforcement or counterintelligence measures – can not be leveraged to dissuade such activities. Rather, it highlights the complexities of the strategic ICT environment whereby sovereign powers are particularly susceptible to foreign intervention in their internal affairs. In fact, fixation on defining the precise threshold for a digital act of war (beyond the de facto effects-based analysis to be applied in any actual scenario) distracts from the important question of how cyber operations are actually being used today. They tend to occur in one of four types: (i) operational preparation of the environment for use during future kinetic military conflict (wherein the question of a digital act of war trigger would be much less relevant); (ii) espionage (which is not addressed by public international law); (iii) criminal activity by non-state actors (which is not the usual basis for declarations of war or military reprisals); and (iv) willful intervention below the threshold of armed conflict.

My experience as an intelligence analyst has led me to believe that most adversaries use cyber operations as a strategic alternative to armed conflict and intend to conduct such activities with the deliberate objective of avoiding military retaliation by their targets. The famous strategist Sun Tzu would applaud the use of such means to accomplish one's goals without engaging in costly combat. To concentrate predominantly on the issue of what constitutes an act of war in cyberspace largely misses the strategic appeal of asymmetric cyber capabilities. The entire purpose of many cyber operations is to exert coercive influence without engendering an international armed conflict.

A more worthy focus might be considering what progress has been achieved to date in establishing rules, norms of behavior, or confidence building measures for actions in cyberspace. 2015-16 was a benchmark year for non-binding diplomatic expressions of proposed rules of behavior (i.e. norms) for state actors in cyberspace. In July 2015, a United Nations Group of Governmental Exports (GGE) report was issued that not only reaffirmed the applicability of international law and the United Nations Charter to activities in cyberspace, but also recommended several normative principles – most notably for limiting cyber attacks against civilian critical infrastructures.[5] In September 2015, Presidents Obama and Xi reached an accord to proscribe state-sponsored cyber espionage for commercial gain, which was later embraced by the Group of 20 (G-20) leaders in their joint statement from November 2015.[6] Finally, in March 2016, the Organization for Security and Co-operation in Europe (OSCE) issued its decision on confidence building measures to reduce the risk of ICT conflicts.[7]

While those expressions can be politically expedient and may contribute to the formation of customary international law over lengthy periods of time, one must nonetheless query what – if anything – has changed in the actual behaviors of cyber actors since those diplomatic pronouncements. I would offer that some nations may have altered their modus operandi or adjusted their target sets to some degree, but that the overall security of cyberspace has not been appreciably strengthened. In fact, one can make a reasoned argument that cyberspace is an increasingly contested, vulnerable, and volatile environment despite those diplomatic overtures. To my knowledge, no nation – not even the United States or our closest allies – has declared a sincere interest in outlawing the use of any particular cyber capability under all circumstances. Instead, prohibitive discussions have mainly centered on types of targets that are to be avoided where possible, which although consistent with the effects-based approach mentioned above does little in the way of creating tangible incentives for compliance with such rules. For example, despite the normative proposals cited above, private sector utilities (e.g. in the energy sector) and other critical ICT infrastructures remain preferred targets for cyber operators.

International negotiations regarding ICT are unlikely to yield concrete, enforceable rules of behavior in the near term because different nations have fundamentally different political objectives for those discussions. The United States defines cyber security primarily in the context of critical infrastructure protection (i.e. keeping the "pipes" up and running), while nations like Russia and China are equally concerned about regulating the informational content transiting those networks.[8] A failure to appreciate the import of that strategic distinction might lead one to overestimate the potential impact of diplomatic efforts on actual behaviors (overt, clandestine, or covert). In April 2016, the Russian Federation's lead cyber negotiator even expressed that the range of possible compromise achievable within the GGE framework might have been "exhausted" already.[9]

Since no country seems genuinely eager to forego its sovereign prerogative to develop offensive ICT capabilities and/or conduct cyber operations for national advantage, the international community is left with a Hobbesian paradigm wherein the infamous adage from the Melian Dialogue rings true, namely: "The strong do what they can, and the weak suffer what they must." Given that unsettling reality, further inquiry into the causes of that systemic result is warranted.

The burden of proof currently lies with the victim to establish definitive attribution for an adverse cyber incident. Attribution has two essential components, and any policy decision to publicly attribute an incident (if positive attribution can be established) must be based on three additional considerations. As NIO/Cyber, I advocated a dualistic approach that included both technical attribution (i.e. forensic investigation of the victim's ICT networks, reverse engineering of malicious software code, etc.) and analytic attribution (i.e. an all-source intelligence assessment of potential perpetrators, their possible motivations, the geo-political context, and other expected indicators that might support each hypothesis). Detailed analysis and comparison of historic cyber events illustrate that different types of actors conduct different kinds of operations against different kinds of targets. Each has its own motivations and concerns which necessarily influence what kind of effects it perpetrates and/or what it does with any stolen data. For example, one would expect the "take" from a state sponsored theft of PII from a healthcare of financial institution to be handled much differently than if the same target had been compromised by a criminal element seeking to maximize the monetary value of that information. A holistic attribution assessment must take all of these factors (technical and contextual) into consideration.

Despite significant advances by both public and private sector cyber security researchers in recent years, it still remains difficult to reach high-confidence attribution assessments within the "real time" parameters that would be required for executive decision making during an incident.[10] That necessarily leaves one in a post hoc reactive mode, and even if one eventually reaches an attribution determination, then the next grouping of considerations comes into play.

Any decision regarding whether or not to publicly attribute a cyber event must account for (1) the bilateral and/or multilateral political ramifications of making such an accusation, (2) the relative costs and benefits of disclosing the evidence required to substantiate an attribution statement, and (3) whether or not one is willing and/or able to punish the perpetrator to whom the event is to be attributed. In this regard, the political decision about the merits of public attribution is wholly independent from the underlying factual question about attribution. One can easily imagine scenarios where one nation may not choose to publicly confront an ally, a trading partner, or a key creditor nation. But, the dilemmas posed by the second and third considerations are even more difficult.

Cyberspace is possibly unique in that the victims of adverse events have a very strong incentive not to publicly prove what has been done to them and by whom. That is owing to the fact that the very same kinds of ICT, methodologies, and accesses that are used for cyber intelligence operations are also used for cyber attack operations. Accordingly, a revelation of evidence that could compromise sources and methods for future intelligence collection might also enable an adversary to develop countermeasures for national military capabilities as well. In other contexts, such as the nuclear model, the technological platforms for intelligence and reconnaissance are distinct from the platforms required for a retaliatory strike. Strategically speaking, no such bifurcation of platforms exists in the cyber arena – which in turn provides a strong disincentive, or at least a very high threshold, for any nation's willingness to "prove" an attribution assessment for the international community writ large.

Another strategic consideration for public attribution relates to global power dynamics. If a nation has declared certain offenses to be unacceptable and announces that one has occurred, its reputation and the credibility of its deterrent mechanisms are then put to the test. Therefore, one can infer that nations might not wish to publicly attribute events for which they know they cannot exact satisfaction. And that dilemma is only exacerbated by the fact, mentioned above, that cyber capabilities are perishable once revealed. There is no analogue to a standing navy in port or intercontinental ballistic missile silo whose mere existence serves as a credible deterrent. In essence, today's cyber strategist would not be inclined to disclose specific offensive cyber capabilities unless she was prepared to use them imminently. Once again, the clear disincentives to publicize retaliatory capabilities or declaratory redlines – and even to prove that one was victimized – all render the cyber dialogue uncharacteristic of other strategic policy discussions.

High-confidence, public attribution remains one of the most pertinent topics in international cyber conferences. On the one hand, it seems like a natural prerequisite for any legitimate accusation or reprisal. But, on the other hand, the technical realities of cyberspace currently permit offenders to either evade punishment (based on insufficient public attribution) or else inflict further policy dilemmas and security compromises on the already afflicted victim.

The market for cyber intelligence has grown propitiously. Governments around the world now benefit from thousands of cyber security analysts in the private sector who are monitoring networks, remediating incidents, and investigating breaches around the clock. Private companies are also increasingly providing threat intelligence that is steadily approaching the all-source format used by governmental intelligence agencies and security services. Personally, I welcome that expanded industry focus from a defender's perspective even though I must also acknowledge that it complicates certain US military, intelligence, counterintelligence, and law enforcement missions.

The private sector already owns and operates much of the critical infrastructure in the United States. It is also increasingly positioned to provide cyber threat intelligence and high quality attribution assessments. And private companies are also increasingly being targeted by a broad range of illicit cyber actors, whether as part of geo-political conflicts or by profit-motivated criminals. Any public policy discussions regarding cyber deterrence, norms of behavior, or strategic implications for US national and economic security that do not take account of private sector input should be considered lacking. That is not to say that the US Government should defer to corporations on sovereign matters, but rather that it must acknowledge that it no longer leads technological innovation for the nation or suffers the primary brunt of conflicts in cyberspace.

Another interesting observation from my analytic outreach to many industry professionals and academic international relations theorists over the years has been the centrality of improved resiliency for maintaining the fullest breadth of one's own national security policy options. As the preceding discussion about attribution and credible deterrents alluded, the weaker one's own cyber capabilities are, the more limited one's policy options will be in the face of an adversary's transgression. So it is very noteworthy, albeit counterintuitive, that a strong cyber offense requires an equally strong if not stronger cyber defense. That is what permits the freedom of maneuver.

In the case of the United States, that represents a call for improved cyber security practices across public utilities and other critical infrastructures throughout multiple sectors. It remains unclear if legislation, regulation, or market forces will eventually induce the desired result. It also remains unclear how US-based multinational corporations will navigate an increasingly complex environment of data privacy, data retention, encryption, event disclosure, and surveillance laws from multiple jurisdictions (both domestic and foreign). In the interim, I envision that the nascent cyber insurance market, along with heightened reporting requirements for data breaches or other cyber events by the Securities and Exchange Commission, will begin to incentivize companies towards adopting best practices for cyber security. That will in turn bolster other governmental efforts, such as the Cybersecurity Framework promulgated by the National Institute of Standards and Technology (NIST) at the Department of Commerce.

I cannot purport to have solutions for all of the policy challenges that I have outlined in this Statement; however, with the Subcommittees' indulgence, I will offer some limited recommendations for consideration going forward:

- Concerted thought is required on the strategic realities that would be both necessary and sufficient to create an effective deterrent to foreign and domestic cyber threats. One cannot presume that diplomatic overtures automatically translate into behavioral changes, or that international law will not be honored in the breach.

- New normative frameworks should be considered which accept the prevalence of cyber operations – including against private sector targets during peacetime – and instead focus on holding actors strictly liable for any and all effects (intended or otherwise) caused by their deliberate actions.[11] Some form of enforcement mechanism is required to better constrain offensive cyber activity.

- US policy makers should consider the potential benefits of clear, declaratory redlines in cyberspace as well as the use of overt cyber operations where it is determined that US military or law enforcement action is warranted. The strategic uncertainty in cyberspace is partly owing to the ubiquitous use of clandestine operations to evade attribution and obfuscate sovereign influences.

- Improved cyber defenses and resiliency are required throughout US critical infrastructures in order to provide US policy makers the greatest breadth of policy options when confronted with adversarial events. Perfect cyber security is impossible, so risk mitigation and risk management models must be employed to maintain core operations and enterprise value even in a degraded environment.

- The US private sector should be consulted more thoroughly in connection with national policy decisions whose impact will be borne by those companies. Military and diplomatic strategies that could indirectly harm the US economy by imposing additional transaction costs, inducing foreign retaliation against US companies, or concealing dangerous vulnerabilities that can be exploited by our adversaries should receive careful review.

- Public agencies in the United States face extreme challenges in recruiting and retaining world class ICT talent. Cyber expertise is a qualitative vice quantitative endeavor (i.e. the number of congressionally authorized billets matters less than who is filling those billets). Additional consideration should be given to ensuring that the US Government employs more of the cyber "Olympians".

Once again, thank you for this opportunity to provide service to my country.

Respectfully submitted by Sean Kanuck.

[1] See: James R. Clapper, Director of National Intelligence, Statement for the Record, Worldwide Threat Assessment of the US Intelligence Community, Senate Select Committee on Intelligence, 12 March 2013; James R. Clapper, Director of National Intelligence, Statement for the Record, Worldwide Threat Assessment of the US Intelligence Community, Senate Select Committee on Intelligence, 29 January 2014; James R. Clapper, Director of National Intelligence, Statement for the Record, Worldwide Threat Assessment of the US Intelligence Community, Senate Armed Services Committee, 26 February 2015; and James R. Clapper, Director of National Intelligence, Statement for the Record, Worldwide Threat Assessment of the US Intelligence Community, Senate Armed Services Committee, 9 February 2016.

[2] For discussion regarding points (a) and (b), see Sean Kanuck, "Sovereign Discourse on Cyber Conflict Under International Law" in Texas Law Review, Volume 88, Number 7, June 2010 (pages 1573-1580). For discussion regarding point (c), see James R. Clapper, Director of National Intelligence, Statement for the Record, Worldwide Threat Assessment of the US Intelligence Community, Senate Select Committee on Intelligence, 12 March 2013 (page 1). For discussion regarding point (d), see James R. Clapper, Director of National Intelligence, Statement for the Record, Worldwide Threat Assessment of the US Intelligence Community, Senate Armed Services Committee, 26 February 2015 (page 1).

[3] See Sean P. Kanuck, "Information Warfare: New Challenges for Public International Law" in Harvard International Law Journal, Volume 37, Number 1, Winter 1996 (page 292). See generally, Michael N. Schmitt, "Computer Network Attack and the Use of Force in International Law: Thoughts on a Normative Framework" in Columbia Journal of Transnational Law, Volume 37, 1999.

[4] See generally, Tallinn Manual on the International Law Applicable to Cyber Warfare, North Atlantic Treaty Organization (NATO) Cooperative Cyber Defence Centre of Excellence, 15 March 2013.

[5] See "Group of Governmental Experts on Developments in the Field of Information and Telecommunications in the Context of International Security", United Nations General Assembly document A/70/174, 22 July 2015. See also, "Group of Governmental Experts on Developments in the Field of Information and Telecommunications in the Context of International Security", United Nations General Assembly document A/68/98, 24 June 2013.

[6] See the White House press release entitled "Fact Sheet: President Xi Jinping's State Visit to the United States" dated 25 September 2015, and the "G20 Leaders' Communiqué" from the Antalya Summit held on 15-16 November 2015.

[7] See Decision Number 1202 of the Permanent Council of the Organization for Security and Co-operation in Europe entitled "OSCE Confidence-Building Measures to Reduce the Risks of Conflict Stemming from the Use of Information and Communication Technologies" dated 10 March 2016. See also Decision Number 1106 of the Permanent Council of the Organization for Security and Co-operation in Europe entitled "Initial Set of OSCE Confidence-Building Measures to Reduce the Risks of Conflict Stemming from the Use of Information and Communication Technologies" dated 3 December 2013.

[8] See generally: White House press release regarding Presidential Policy Directive/PPD-21 entitled "Critical Infrastructure Security and Resilience" dated 12 February 2013; Executive Order 13636 of 12 February 2013 entitled "Improving Critical Infrastructure Cybersecurity" in Federal Register, Volume 78, Number 33, 19 February 2013; United Nations General Assembly document A/69/723, Annex entitled "International code of conduct for information security", 13 January 2015; and Shanghai Cooperation Organization, Agreement between the Governments of the Member States of the Shanghai Cooperation Organization on Cooperation in the Field of International Information Security, 16 June 2009.

[9] Statement made by Andrey Krutskikh to US Government officials on the margins of the United Nations Institute for Disarmament (UNIDIR) workshop entitled "The Application of International Law in the Context of International Cybersecurity" held in Geneva, Switzerland from 19-21 April 2016.

[10] See generally, James R. Clapper, Director of National Intelligence, Statements for the Record, Worldwide Threat Assessment of the US Intelligence Community, Senate Armed Services Committee, 9 February 2016 (page 3) and 26 February 2015 (page 2).

[11] See e.g., proposed norm number 22 in The Hague Centre for Strategic Studies working paper for the Global Conference on Cyber Security entitled "Food for thought for break-out group 'Confidence Building Measures, Norms of Behavior and Public-Private Cooperation for International Security in Cyberspace'" presented on 17 April 2015 in The Hague, Netherlands.

Mr. HURD. Thank you, Mr. Kanuck.

Mr. Singer, you are now recognized for 5 minutes.

STATEMENT OF PETER WARREN SINGER

Mr. SINGER. Mr. Chairman, Ranking Members, and members of the subcommittee, it's an honor to speak at this important discussion today designed to reboot the cybersecurity conversation. This shift is direly needed as there is perhaps no national security problem more 21st century in its definition and form than cybersecurity, and yet, to solve it, too much of our discussion and strategy remains rooted in 20th century frameworks that don't well apply.

I've submitted written testimony that breaks down the issue and what we can do about it. It focuses on the debate over digital acts of war and explains in detail how there are seven key differences with the cold war that make framing this problem in the old modes not ideal. It then provides a suggested new legislative strategy to face our challenge, breaking it down into key areas I'll focus on today.

Notably, the strategy is nonpartisan, realistic in its implementation possibilities, and doesn't involve any massive increase in budget.

The first key part of the strategy is deter through diversity. This includes improving our offensive cyber capability, but importantly, understanding that cyber weapons are not like WMD. They are tools of constant use in everything from espionage to ongoing operations against ISIS.

Our real challenge here is more in integrating emerging cyber capabilities with our other conventional capabilities through improving training, doctrine building, and resolving command and control questions.

But as we face an array of attacks and attackers, a military offensive cyber response is not the only tool that we have to change their calculations. For instance, to respond to IP theft, it makes no sense to limit ourselves to retaliation with the exact same action in the same domain. We can also go after other assets that are valued by the attacker in other realms and even those valued by influential third party actors, such as sanctioning companies benefitting from stolen fruit.

Indictments of individuals involved in hacking have value not so much in actual direct judicial punishment, but as a different means for surfacing data about attribution. Creativity and flexibility will beat simplicity in this dynamic. Indeed, we may even steal ideas from one attacker's playbook and apply them against another as a deterrence tool.

From Snowden to Sony, data dumps have been among our most vexing cybersecurity incidents, but they have not threatened our core national interests. By contrast, threatening to reveal the private financial data of an authoritarian regime's leader, his family, or allied oligarchs may be far more potent than a counter cyber strike. We can sometimes see what regimes fear most by what they ban discussion of.

The second and arguably most important part of the strategy is deterrence by denial, making attacks less likely to cause harm, and thus, less likely to happen. The magic word of resilience is that it works against any kind of attacker and attack, and it's perhaps where Congress and this committee can have the most impact.

The areas that call out for action cover the spectrum. On the military side, we have spent over $2 billion on construction alone at Fort Meade, and yet the Pentagon's own weapons tester found, quote, "significant vulnerabilities," end quote, in nearly every major weapon system program that would be exploited in any actual war.

In the executive branch, the White House has issued a post-OPM cybersecurity strategy that describes best practices every Federal agency needs to put in place. Ensuring their actual implementation at every Federal Government agency and encouraging their spread to the State and local level could be one of the most important things that Congress does on cybersecurity.

In relation to the business and public, sometimes government can be a trusted information provider and sometimes it must go further to help shape individual and market incentives, as it has in realms that range from public health to transportation. The government should not merely support research on basic standards of Internet security, such as the laudable NIST process, but now work to ensure their use. It can do so by efforts to spur the nascent cybersecurity insurance market that both protects business and incentivizes them to find and maintain best practices.

True cybersecurity resilience is not just about computer and legal code. It's also about people, and we have a huge people gap here. The administration has a new Cybersecurity Human Resources Strategy, but it needs to, one, be overseen to ensure actual implementation, particularly across administrations, and two, it will fail if it only puts new people in old organizational boxes.

We also have to find ways to tap talent outside of government. Take the Pentagon's recent 1 month experiment with bug bounties. It saved millions of dollars, yielded 1,100 reports on how to protect our systems before the bad guys could attack them, and it talent scouted across the U.S. One of the hackers working for us was an 18-year-old who did it in his spare time while taking his AP exams. Yet there is not a parallel at other Federal agencies, nor at our State and local partners.

Or consider that we have retasked a number of National Guard units to become cyber warriors, but there is a wealth of talent that is either unwilling or unable to meet the legal and physical obligations that come with joining the U.S. military. Here I would point to Estonia's Cyber Defense League as a model to draw on. Think of it as the cybersecurity equivalent to the Civil Air Patrol, creating a mechanism for citizens to volunteer their expertise for cybersecurity to aid—for free—in everything from red teaming to serving as rapid response teams to cyber attack. They have helped Estonia become one of the most cyber-resilient nations in the world.

The third role of the strategy, I won't hit. It's norms. It's in the submission. I think it's been covered well here.

I would end just simply by saying we can either approach this topic with a new strategy that faces our new needs or we can continue to talk tough and simple and be victims.

Thank you.
[Prepared statement of Mr. Singer follows:]

Prepared Testimony and Statement for the Record of

P.W. Singer
Strategist at New America

At the

Hearing on "Digital Acts of War."

Before the House Committee on Oversight and Government Reform
Joint IT and National Security Subcommittee

July 13, 2016

Chairmen Hurd and DeSantis, Ranking Members Kelly and Lynch, and Members of the Subcommittees, thank you for the opportunity to testify before the committee today.

My name is Peter W. Singer. I am Strategist at New America, a non-partisan thinktank with a goal of preparing the US for the new digital age; the author of a variety of books on security, including <u>Cybersecurity and Cyberwar: What Everyone Needs to Know</u>, a primer on cybersecurity issues, and <u>Ghost Fleet</u>, which is a look at the future of war; and the co-host of the Cybersecurity podcast, which Chairman Hurd was kind enough to join us for an interview last year. It is an honor to speak at this important discussion today, designed to reboot the cybersecurity conversation.

There is perhaps no national security problem more 21st century in both its definition and form than cybersecurity. And yet to solve it, the ready solution in nearly every U.S. national security conversation today is the 20th-century framework of Cold War style deterrence. It argues that the best way to stop the frustrating array of cyberattacks on the United States -- ranging from credit card theft, to <u>emails stolen</u> from Hollywood studios, to the millions of <u>security clearance records</u> lifted from the Office of Personnel Management (OPM), to not yet realized fears of a national power grid collapses or devastating military defeat through digital means-- is to demonstrate the capability and willingness to hit back just as hard.

This rhetoric of achieving Cold War deterrence by retaliation is appealing. It offers both simplicity, an easy answer that echoes back to a time of familiarity, and the allure of a rhetoric that seemingly demonstrates strength and resolve.

There is just one problem: Any cybersecurity strategy based on merely whacking back to end hacking is not going to work. This is a new technology and a new era, and U.S. deterrence thinking needs to reflect our new needs.

Not Your Grandfather's Deterrence: Why the Cold War Parallels Fail

In the Cold War, the challenge was huge, but the problem was relatively simple. The opposing sides possessed roughly the same type and number of weapons, and these weapons affected them both in roughly the same way. The attack to be deterred was a clear and obvious one, with clear attribution that assured mutual and equal destruction in a massive mushroom cloud. Thus, building up a potent offense, and being willing and able to use it, translated directly into deterrence.

Today, though, there are seven key differences that mean the Cold War model of deterrence is not an apt one to deal with the threats of a new digital world.

First is the different civilian versus military makeup of the issue. In the Cold War, while support of the population mattered, the basic competition of deterrence came down to the two sides' defense and strategic nuclear establishments. Today, the domain in question is civilian-owned and operated (even 98% of US military communications go over civilian systems), meaning everything from the technology itself is to many of the most important players are civilian, from the protectors (civilian government agencies like the FBI and DHS to cybersecurity firms) to the targets themselves (civilian agencies like the OPM or NASA to the individual victims of over $1 Trillion in cybercrime).

The relative position of the military and civilian world is also reversed. In the Cold War, the military led the way, including even funding the creation of the Internet itself. Today, it is the civilian world that is often doing cutting-edge work in everything from finding new zero days to building new means of encryption. This applies even to the human resources side. There was no private market in the Cold War for missileers in the same way that there is a booming cybersecurity industry that rivals and sometimes surpasses talent inside of the military, as well as makes it harder to retain.

Second, today, there is no "mutual" to balance, let alone "assured" nature of any action, nor "destruction" of the same scale. The United States is arguably more vulnerable to cyberattack than any of its adversaries, largely because of its wide commercial, military, and cultural dependence on the Internet. This feels daunting, but is, on balance, a good thing. North Korea, for instance, may be in the seemingly enviable position of being the world's least vulnerable nation to cyberattack. But this seeming strength comes at the cost of global isolation, dictatorship, and an <u>economy</u> that relies on military-run pig farms.

Likewise, while conventional and nuclear weapons have highly predictable, i.e. "assured," consequences, cyber attacks are uncertain by their very nature. Their impact depends on multiple, often unpredictable actions, and often have second and third orders effects unanticipated by their designers. The (at the time) covert operation to deploy Stuxnet in 2009-2010, for instance, was arguably one of the most successful digital attacks in history, as it successfully sabotaged Iranian nuclear research equipment. Yet, the software was discovered as it popped up in some 25,000 other computers located around the world, from Belarus to India, contrary to the operational plan.

Finally, while there are great threats and costs from cyber attack, no human has yet been directly hurt or killed by one. Of the very few attacks that have caused physical impact (three are most commonly recognized at this time: Stuxnet, the 2015 Ukrainian power grid hack, and a suspected attack in 2014 at a <u>German steel factory</u>), the actual destructive damage has so far been limited to less than a grenade could do, let alone the Hiroshima device. Looking forward, we can envision cyber attacks that would cause great physical damage and even death, such as the take down of a city or even entire region's power grid. Yet, even in such worst fears, the death toll would still be orders of magnitude smaller than the toll of a single nuclear bomb, let alone the all out thermonuclear war between the US and USSR that threatened human existence and thus was truly MAD.

Third, there is an inverse relationship to conventional military strengths and weaknesses that guided us in the past. Underpinning Cold War deterrence strategy was that the United States perceived itself weaker than the Soviet Union in conventional warfighting, worrying about a quick takeover of Western Europe by a larger Red Army. Thus, it relied on the threat of nuclear response to avoid an unequal conventional war. Today, we face an opposite dilemma. It is the United States that has the conventional edge on its adversaries and our attackers see cyberattacks as their asymmetric way to work around a power imbalance. This points to a key aspect in our deterrence today: our willingness and ability to escalate in the opposite direction as the Cold War. If an act in cyberspace is an "act of war,' we retain the option to respond with acts of war in other domains where we may have an even great advantage, with the knowledge of that fact providing an added dose of deterrence.

Fourth, the timing is fundamentally different. The physics of a ballistic missile's speed and arc determined conceptions of deterrence during the Cold War. The critical <u>30 minutes</u> it would take an intercontinental missile to fly across continents was essential to planning and strategy.

In cybersecurity, however, time operates by different rules. While cyberattacks <u>seemingly move at digital speed</u>, the ones that are actually effective take months or years to plan, organize, conduct, and -- most importantly -- detect. An attacker often carries out long periods of preparation and intelligence gathering, all with the goals of gaining and keeping entry. The alleged Chinese OPM hacks that stole sensitive data of over 21 million Americans may be on policymakers' minds now, but the attack actually started as <u>early</u> as March 2014, well over a year before it became an issue of defender or Congressional awareness. Indeed, <u>the average time</u> it takes a victim of a cyber attack to detect that they have been breached is 205 days. In its study of APT1, a hacking campaign linked to the Chinese People's Liberation Army (PLA) Unit 61398, the security firm Mandiant <u>found that</u> the unit spent as long as 5 years undetected inside several of its targets' networks.

It is not just about preparation or detection; the timeline of reaction is also fundamentally different. As opposed to the need to act within the tight, 30-minute window of Cold War missiles, in cybersecurity the defender's best move may well not be to strike back as rapidly as possible, but to show no outside awareness of the ongoing attack. This complicates the attacker's damage assessments. It even allows the victim to turn the tables and steer the attacker into areas where they cannot do harm, or feed them false information that undermines their whole endeavor.

The weapons also come with different timelines -- not just in their creation, but also in their utility. The <u>Minuteman</u> Intercontinental Ballistic Missile (ICBM) was conceived in 1956, and served as the central tool of U.S. nuclear deterrence for the next three decades of the Cold War. But its utility did not stop there. Indeed, roughly 450 Minuteman III missiles <u>still protect</u> the United States today, with plans for them to serve to 2030 or even beyond. By contrast, the most dangerous cyberweapons depend on new "zero days" -- vulnerabilities the victim is not yet aware of. Yet, what is most potent today, a single software patch can render inert tomorrow.

Fifth is a fundamental difference in the players of the game itself, in their makeup, number, and interests. The actors who the United States is supposed to be cyber deterring are far more diverse than the Cold War list that included only the Soviet Union (which notably had a fairly similar power status and even nuclear doctrine). More than 60 countries <u>have</u> cyber-military capabilities, ranging from large and powerful states to weak regimes. Non-state actors also are in the game, and they range from transnational criminals to hacktivist networks to maybe the most difficult of all, proxy groups taking advantage of the grey space in between, sometimes working on behalf of states and sometimes on their own. Moreover, it is not just the different numbers, but that each actor comes with vastly different interests and stakes in the game. Akin to terrorism or crime, some players have assets or positions they greatly value, and thus are deterrable, while some value mere chaos, and thus are not.

Sixth, as diverse as the players are, another difference is the diversity of attacks they might carry out. Those vary from theft of intellectual property to <u>online dumps</u> of embarrassing Hollywood studio emails, to the (not yet realized) risks of a massive kinetic attack on critical infrastructure, such as using Stuxnet style digital weaponry against industrial control systems to collapse power grids or transportation networks. So when people talk today about their fears that US cyber deterrence has failed, they are both right and wrong. Not every kind of attack is being thwarted, yet the worst kind of attack that major states are capable of are indeed being deterred.

This variety reinforces a key aspect in the discussion of digital war: not all attacks in constitute an act of war. They range from acts of theft to protest to espionage that ranges from sabotage to subversion to the fear of an actual act of war, traditionally defined as political violence on a mass scale. The stealing of a secret, for instance, is vexing, but no nation has ever gone to war over such an event. Such distinctions are important not just in defining what is and isn't war, but also what is and isn't a US military responsibility. If every cyber threat becomes a military issue, not only is that inefficient in term of applying the right response, but it also over burdens an already busy US military.

While attribution is often identified as a central problem in cybersecurity and acts of war discussions -- unlike an ICBM, a cyberattack does not emit a clear plume of smoke to identify the attacker -- the existence of diverse attackers and diverse attacks muddies the water further: it can be incredibly complicated to determine the intent of an attack, even if its form and sender are known. When a <u>Russian criminal group</u> with ties to Russian intelligence was detected attacking U.S. banks in 2014, for instance, the security community debated whether it was regular old cybercrime, or an attack linked to Russian state interests, designed as a response to the sanctioning of the regime for its invasion of Ukraine. But even then, was the attack a retaliation that got caught? Or was it akin to a nuclear test in a crisis, a signal that was actually intended to be detected, as a warning of greater consequences if the United States pushed further?

The problem of comparison when it comes attack types does not stop there. Unlike in the Cold War, some cyber attacks that target the United States are the kind of attacks that we would actually like to carry out ourselves, or, in fact, already do. US Military and White

House officials reacted far more mildly to the OPM email breach than many in the public expected. Why? In part, it is because attacks targeting a government agency's networks are the bread and butter of the online espionage operations the United States implements against other governments. As Director of National Intelligence James Clapper said in June, 2015 after the discovery of the OPM attack, "You have to kind of salute the Chinese for what they did. If we had the opportunity to do that, I don't think we'd hesitate for a minute." When it comes to attacks like on the OPM, instead of telling the attackers "Shame on you," we need to look in the mirror and say "Shame on us for making their job so easy."

Seventh, and perhaps where the Cold War parallels fall short the most, is the idea that building up like offensive capabilities will deliver deterrence. This is a constant refrain: not just the need to build up U.S. cyber offense, but the need to make sure others know the United States has those capabilities. As James Cartwright, the four-star Marine Corps general who led much of the initial U.S. strategy in cyber issues until his retirement in 2011, said, "You can't have something that's a secret be a deterrent. Because if you don't know it's there, it doesn't scare you."

The problem is that the evidence so far disproves this link. Unlike concerns over bomber and missile "gaps" during the Cold War (which instructively turned out to be wrong), the United States' offensive cyberspace capabilities have never been in question. And for anyone somehow in doubt, there have been series of public releases that further confirmed it. These included Washington policymakers' leaks designed to take credit for Stuxnet, and then Edward Snowden's 2014 dump of some 1.4 million NSA documents. While Snowden's disclosures obviously angered his former employers, they also show that the experts at Fort Meade have much to be proud of. The NSA has developed unmatched, amazingly exotic capabilities, from a mindboggling scale of global monitoring devices to new classes of cyber weapons that use radio signals to jump software over the previously protective physical divides between systems. And the leaks show the capability is not mere lab work, but that the NSA has used them in operations against targets ranging from Iranian nuclear research facilities to Chinese command networks.

Yet despite this clear and continual gain in offensive capability and the demonstration of its potency, attacks on the United States have only grown, in both number and in intensity. In the year after the Snowden leaks proved the U.S.'s offensive prowess, there was 55% more data lost from hacking than the year before -- and that does not even include the operations targeting major government sites like OPM or the Pentagon's Joint Staff network that began in that same period.

In sum, the flaw is not with deterrence theory, nor with cyber weapons' utility. Rather, it is with the framing of the problem. We too often try to peel off the bumper-sticker version of complicated Cold War deterrence debates and apply it to a more complicated present and future.

A Deterrence Path Forward

So what to do instead? There are the three better ways for the United States to draw the right lessons from the Cold War and reach more effective and more obtainable cyber deterrence goals.

1) Set the Norms

There is a huge value in delineating clear lines of behavior in a combined commercial, espionage, and warfighting space still at its infancy. During the height of the Cold War, the superpowers may have been a button press away from thermonuclear annihilation, but they still found a way to agree on certain norms. Sometimes these were formal arms treaties; other times they were tacit codes of conduct that guided everything from limiting spy-on-spy killings to avoiding interference with nuclear commands. Cutting across all was the goal of avoiding miscalculations that could unintentionally escalate into outright war.

Today, at the global level, much of the norm discussion in the UN GGE process has been about establishing potential rules of the road for military conflict in cyberspace. Inside US defense and political circles, by contrast, much of cyber deterrence and norm discussions has been on how to end the spate of government-enabled attacks on intellectual property, which was at the center of the agreement hammered out this fall between the United States and China. There is mixed reporting since on the impact of the agreement. The overall number of IP theft attacks are reportedly down, with some crediting the reduction to the agreement, while others credit unrelated forces like domestic Chinese government anti-corruption activities.

What is clear is that three activities will continue. Theft of intellectual property is integral to the Chinese mercantilist economic model, so while the number is down, the overall practice is, and by all indications, will still continue. In turn, the United States is wedded to the open flow of information, but Beijing sometimes interprets platforms that share freedom of speech as "information attacks" that threaten its internal stability. So China will perceive itself under continued attacks of a different kind from the US. And both sides, whose militaries are engaged in an arms race in the Pacific, will continue to engage in espionage to better position themselves if there was outright war.

This dynamic illustrates how reaching a formal prohibition on cyberattacks of any and all kinds between the 21st century powers unlikely. It does not mean, however, that there is no value in engagement and norm building. Rather than a treaty or agreement that unrealistically tries to create a Cold War-style regime of deterrence or arms control, the two sides need to flesh out a mutual understanding of the new rules of the game. Both sides must understand that their opponent will continue to conduct cyberactivities ranging from espionage to theft. The most important goal is not to stop every cyberattack, but to keep them from escalating into something far more dangerous.

This leads to a fundamental change in the typical deterrence discussion. In the Cold War, everything was targeted, from military bases to cities full of civilians, but outright attacks crossed the line. Today, the situation is inverted. While unwanted, some cyberattacks will have to be allowed, while certain targets must be made anathema.

This returns to the point that not all 'cyberattacks' are act of war. No one wants their state secrets stolen, for example, but it is part of the expected dance of great powers in competition. By contrast, there are other attacks that may not be clear acts of war, but they should be a focus on norm building to prohibit, as they make war more likely. Introducing the digital equivalent of a dormant Tasmanian devil into a nuclear power facility's operating system should be off limits to both sides, not merely because it would be disproportional if actually used, but because simply the act of deploying it risks accident or event interpretation as an incredibly escalatory step of preparing for war.

Continuing to set and reinforce these guardrails has to be one of the key activities in the various bilateral and multilateral efforts in this space, from U.S. agreements on cybersecurity with to the two U.N. General Assembly resolutions that call for respect of the laws of war in cyberspace, to the Tallinn Manual process.

Yet, for all the laudable work in building norms, what threatens to undermine norm-building is inaction when acts clearly violate the norms. One of the consistently agreed upon norms is not to target clear civilian infrastructure with the intent to cause widespread damage (as opposed to monitor or steal information), even more so outside of declared war. Such attacks are viewed as violating the norms of necessity and proportionality that underpin the laws of war.

Yet, in December of 2015, this line was clearly crossed in an attack on the Ukrainian power grid. More than 230,000 civilians lost power, in a what has been positively identified as a cyber attack by both local authorities and international experts, and US officials have identified Russia as the attacker (going back to the issue of proxy actors, they have not made clear whether it was government or non government but government linked actors). It was the first proven takedown of a power grid, the long discussed nightmare scenario. Yet, in the story of action and consequence that is the key to maintaining norms, we had clear action, but as yet no clear consequence.

2) Deter Through Diversity

Nothing above argues against building up offensive capabilities for cyberspace. Cyberweapons have proven their value in espionage, sabotage, and conflict. And the digital domain will be as crucial to warfare in the 21st century as operations on land, air, and sea. Indeed, the cyber front of any war between the United States and China would feature not just military units like Cyber Command or the PLA's Unit 61398, but also non-state actors that might range from Chinese university cyber militias to Anonymous hackers joining in the fight with their own goals and modes, much as what has happened in the online ISIS battles.

This is a good illustration of another misperception: Cyberweapons are increasingly useful tools of espionage and war, but they are not akin to "weapons of mass destruction." The fear of a single big thermonuclear tit for tat maintained the nuclear balance; indeed, treating nuclear weapons as no different from conventional weapons is what many feared would unravel MAD. Offensive cyber capabilities, by contrast, are a key part of the toolkit to be used in both hot and cold conflicts. Indeed, the US has already crossed this line by openly admitting to conducting offensive cyber operations against ISIS.

We can and should continue to build our offensive cyber capabilities. The key to their optimal effectiveness, though, will be in doctrine building and integration; i.e. how we meld activities in the cyber domain with conventional operations in the air, sea, land, and space. Achieving ranges from bolstering training and operational planning to clarifying command

and control relationships. Indeed, if there is a historic parallel to worry about, it is not Cold War battles never fought, but a digital version of the 1942 Battle of Kasserine Pass, where a US military failure to bring together technologies and units across domains helped contribute to the early losses of World War II.

That a cyber weapon is not like a WMD does not mean the United States has no options to exact costs on would-be attackers to change their calculations, the goal of deterrence outside of war. Indeed, it may even have more. Just as the timeline is stretched out and the players are proliferated as compared to the Cold War, the options for responding are proliferated. True deterrence building responses can come after the fact and in other realms. For instance, our only option is not to respond to IP theft by taking the exact same action, in the same domain. The defender can also go after other assets valued by the attacker or even those valued by third party actors, from sanctioning companies benefiting from stolen fruit to personal level actions like threatening to revoke valued visas for regime leader family members to attend US schools. Indictments of individuals involved in hacking might serve a purpose not of actual prosecution and punishment, but as a different means of surfacing data about attribution, or to make access to the global financial system more difficult. This dynamism complicates things to a degree that even the most brilliant Cold War strategist would find vexing.

The raised options increase the complexity we have to work through. Leaders will have to game out not merely the first two moves of the response -- the simple "shoot and shoot back" dynamic that was the whole of thinking they needed in any Cold War nuclear exchange -- but plot out moves in multiple stages by multiple actors. For instance, the success of legal or trade sanctions will depend not just on whether a punishment for past attacks would stop future attacks, but also what the United States is prepared and willing to do in response to loss of market access were China, say, to respond in kind against some American firms.

Creativity and flexibility will beat simplicity in this dynamic. Indeed, the United States may even steal ideas from one attacker's playbook as a useful tool against another. From Sony to Snowden, leaked emails and documents have been among the most vexing incidents for cybersecurity. But the irony is that here the lack of mutuality is to our advantage; the U.S.'s system of government and open society is least vulnerable to them. For all the sturm and drang over revelations of questionable metadata collection and Angelina Jolie gossip, U.S. political and societal stability has never been at risk from this practice of what is known as "doxing," Yet, as Catherine Lotrionte at Georgetown University has noted, threatening to reveal the private financial data of a regime's leader, his family, or allied oligarchs, may be far more potent. In thinking through such targeting for cyber deterrence, we can see sometimes see what regimes fear most by what they ban. Witness the different responses to the Panama Papers, which were short-lived news articles of interest in the US, but led the Chinese government to censor discussion of even the word Panama on its social media.

Across all these efforts, the goal is not to prevent all attacks, like MAD did with nuclear weapons. Rather, it is to change the potential attacker's calculus on whether an individual cyberattack will be beneficial in the final tally.

3) Shake It Off: Build Resilience

The third, most apt lesson from a deeper dive into the Cold War deterrence debates is the value not just in raising the costs, but also in limiting the adversary's potential gains. This is known as "deterrence by denial" -- making attacks less likely by reducing their likely value. In today's parlance, this is the crucial idea of "resilience." If Congress wants to evolve the cybersecurity conversation, it should move resilience to the center of it.

In both strategy and football, sometimes the best defense is a good defense. A half-century ago, strategic planners did not just talk about striking back as the key to deterrence, <u>but also</u> on having "survivable" counter or "second strike" missiles that would nuke the other side, even if it tried a sneak attack. This is why the United States put missiles on expensive submarines and in hardened siloes.

Resilience today is about creating the capacity to power through an attack and <u>shake it off</u>, thereby limiting the gains to the attacker and recovering rapidly from any losses. Building resilience is not as politically appealing as striking back with new cyberweapons, because it means accepting that this is a digital world where the risk of cyberattacks is not going away. Yet it is more realistic, as well as where the United States would be getting far more deterrence bang for its buck. Most importantly to the problem we face in the diversity of cyber problems, it is useful for responding to them all. The great value of building resilience is that it applies to any kind of attacker and any kind of attack.

Unfortunately, despite the attention, rhetoric, and money the United States government spends on cybersecurity, it is still far from resilient against cyber attack. For every gain, there is still a major gap to be closed. In the military, the <u>construction budget</u> alone for Fort Meade, the combined headquarters of the NSA and Cyber Command, will reach $2 billion by the end of 2016, and the force will add another 4,000 personnel. Yet, the Pentagon's own tester still found <u>"significant vulnerabilities"</u> in nearly every major weapons program.

In the broader federal government, the cybersecurity budget for 2016 is 35 percent <u>higher</u> than it was just two years ago. Yet half of security professionals in these agencies <u>think</u> cybersecurity did not improve over that same period. The reasons range from continued failure to follow basic measures – the requirement for personal identification verification cards dates back to 2004 but still is not fully implemented -- to a failure to take seriously the long-term nature of the threats we face, most importantly in a world of renewed geopolitical competition. The exemplar of these failures was the OPM, which dealt with some of the most sensitive government information, and yet <u>outsourced</u> IT work to contractors in China -- despite warnings going back to 2009.

In October, the White House <u>issued</u> a post-OPM "Cybersecurity Strategy and Implementation Plan" that describes a key series of steps that every federal agency needs to take. It included the basic measures that should have been in place long ago: from identifying high-value assets that need to be protected, to accelerating the deployment of detection systems. Ensuring the implementation of these steps could be one of the most important things that Congress could do on cybersecurity. Indeed, it would likely matter more than passage of the much ballyhooed cybersecurity information sharing bill. While the bill had many laudable aspects, 87% of cybersecurity experts <u>think it will not affect</u> the number of major security breaches.

This same uneven implementation plays out across industry. While corporate boards are now talking far more about the problem, cybersecurity spending as a portion of IT budgets is still roughly a quarter of the rate within government IT budgets, while only 25% of key industry players, for example, participated last year in Information Sharing and Analysis Centers (ISACs), which share needed cyber threat data -- the same percentage as in 2014. The outcome is that some sectors, like banking, take cybersecurity seriously, while others, like health care, manufacturing, and infrastructure, remain behind the curve. Of note to the concerns over Ukraine power grid attack is that despite this real demonstration of the risks, experts worry that US companies have not implemented key steps to better protect themselves, not just against the tactics used in December, but how they will naturally evolve in the future.

This concern extends down to the personal level. Unlike in the Cold War, individuals both face personalized cyber threats, but also can contribute more to national security. During the Cold War, "duck and cover" was about all that a population could do when it came to nuclear deterrence. Today, the vast majority of Americans use the Internet, and they can actually make a difference in its defense. Over 90% of cyber attacks would be stopped by basic measures of cyber hygiene, from two factor authentication on accounts to using different passwords for their bank accounts and fantasy football teams.

How this ties together to Congress's role in evolving the cybersecurity conversation is that *we have to rethink the role that government can play in linking cybersecurity policy, markets, and citizenry's behavior.* In other words, government can and should play the role it plays in cybersecurity that it does in other realms, from health to transportation.

Sometimes government can be a trusted provider of useful information to both business and the wider public. And sometimes it can go further to help shape individual and market incentives. For instance, the government created Center for Disease Control (CDC) to fill key gaps, funding research on under-studied diseases, and serving as a trusted exchange for information provided by groups ranging from universities to drug companies. A cyber CDC could meet some of the same needs in cybersecurity.

Similarly, U.S. buildings are filled with "EXIT" signs and fire extinguishers, while cars have seatbelts and crash bags. These demonstrate the efficacy of government in creating *both* voluntary standards and actual regulations to increase security. These regulations are then bolstered by insurance laws and markets that use the combined power of the public and private sector to incentivize good behavior and best practices. Such a system has positively shaped everything from building construction to driving habits.

So too, the government should support not merely research on the basic standards of Internet security , like the laudable NIST process, but now work to backstop them with the nascent cybersecurity insurance market. If Congress can aid in spurring that market to further develop, it can potentially have a massively positive effect on national security.

Last year, the cybersecurity marketplace collected $1.6 billion in premiums. It sounds like much, but is a drop in the bucket compared to the overall scale of the insurance industry (which collected over a trillion dollars comparatively), the scale of our digital economy, and the scale of cybersecurity risk at both a personal, business, and national security level. Less than half of the Fortune 500 have insurance protecting them against cyber incidents (and, in turn, incentivizing and guiding them to undertake best practices to avoid and mitigate these risks), while among mid-sized firms, some 18,000 firms are not yet insured. The protections are also varied across sectors. Much as how banks were among the first to information share and adapt other best cybersecurity practices, so too here are other sectors behind; only 5% of US manufacturing firms have cyber insurance.

As Elana Broitman explores in her New America report on the needs of a cyber-legislative agenda, Congress can aid in injecting more life into this marketplace. We are certainly not at the point yet in the debate to where such insurance should be required, but Congress can 1) hold hearings to better understand the field and draw attention to its possibilities, 2) help establish an Insurance Laboratory within the National Institute of Standards and Technology (NIST) cybersecurity process, 3) work with the industry and state partners to encourage the building of common cybersecurity insurance industry terms and language, something that requires regulatory cooperation across states, thus fitting with Congress's constitutional role; and 4) explore the passage of a Cyber equivalent to the Terrorism risk insurance cap (TRIA). Just as such legislation was designed to encourage best practices in protecting infrastructure from conventional terrorism threats post 9-11, the same kind of back stop against catastrophic cyber attacks against critical infrastructure sector (particularly from states in the event of war) would help encourage the spread of insurance that would, not so ironically, help make cyber attacks both less painful and less likely.

The challenge in building true cybersecurity resilience is not only about software and legal code, however, but also about people. Across government and industry, there is a growing lack of cybersecurity professionals; the consultancy Frost and Sullivan estimates that the global gap between security openings and skilled people to fill them will reach 1.5 million by 2020. Thus, even when positions are created and funded, they are difficult to fill, both in private industry and in government. For example, at last report, 40% of the cybersecurity positions at the Federal Bureau of Investigation (FBI) remained unfilled, leaving many field offices without expertise. Diversity is also a problem; less than 10 percent of cybersecurity professionals are women, lower than the already dismal rates in the broader IT world. How can we fill key gaps if we are only recruiting well from less than half the population?

The administration's work in creating a "Cybersecurity Human Resources Strategy" is another of the new, and much needed, milestones in building greater resilience by targeting gaps with scholarship programs and other incentives. But it will fail if it only puts new people in old organizational boxes, using the same pipelines.

Attracting more talented civilian expertise into the government can aid in an overall national strategy, by supporting a "deterrence by denial" strategy across broader networks. Consider, for instance, that after the embarrassment of the healthcare.gov rollout, the government created a Digital Service to bring young Silicon Valley innovators into government to do things like fix the federal health care website design. Even after the OPM debacle, however, there is still not a parallel one to shore up cybersecurity.

Here again, Congress can rewrite the conversation by pulling from best practices that bring together the public and private sector in a manner that cuts across traditional partisan lines.

A good illustration is the Pentagon's recent adaption of a "bug bounty" program. This is a program that offers small rewards (The Pentagon program rewards ranged from $100 to $15,000 for a person that identified multiple security gaps) to encourage a "crowd sourced" solution to cybersecurity; in essence it enlists the ingenuity of citizens to find the holes in our security before the bad guys do. The Pentagon's experiment with this project has been a success. Its first bug reports came in just <u>13 minutes</u> after the contest started. After just 1 month, <u>1410 outside hackers</u> had submitted 1189 reports to help to spot and fix vulnerabilities in the Pentagon's websites.

The cost was $150,000, an order of magnitude at least cheaper than if it had been contracted out, but the gains of the program were also about identifying and building out ties to cybersecurity talent beyond government. For example, one of the hackers who helped defend our military's IT systems via this program was <u>18 year old David Dworken</u>, who did it during his high school AP exams. Congress could play a powerful role in aiding and encouraging the spread of such programs to other federal government agencies, as well as across state and local government partners and private industry.

Similarly, innovations are needed in our military organizational models. Several National Guard units <u>have been retasked</u> to focus on cybersecurity. They have performed admirably, even besting some active duty Cyber Command units in wargames. But the new units only serve as a means to organize talent already serving in the military. There is a far deeper and wider pool of talent outside the military that is simply not going to be accessed by this effort-- either because the individuals are unwilling to meet the various obligations that come with military service (an IT tech in the National Guard, for example, is still legally obligated to serve in any mission they are ordered to, whether it be a cyber 911, Haiti Earthquake response, or Iraq war) or because they are unable to meet the various physical or <u>legal requirements</u> for joining the military.

Here again, there are lessons to be learned from the past that are not usually part of our present day cyber deterrence discussions. During the Cold War, nations like Switzerland or China followed a different strategy, choosing an "active defense" model that was based on deterring attack not by massive retaliation but by mobilizing their citizenry for broader national defense. The United States was in a far different position in the Cold War, so this model was not an apt one for us in the nuclear age. Today in the new issue of cybersecurity, there is much to learn from others, past and present, as they wrestle with similar problems. Estonia's Cyber Defense League, for example, is a particularly <u>good model</u>. Rather than a traditional military reserve, it is more akin to the U.S. Civil Air Patrol, where citizens can build up their own aviation skills, but also volunteer to aid government in aviation-related emergencies. Just in this case, it is a mechanism for Estonian citizens to volunteer their expertise for cybersecurity. They aid in everything from "red teaming" -- finding vulnerabilities in systems and activities before the bad guys can exploit them -- to serving as rapid response teams to cyberattacks. Notably, the members are not just technical experts; the needed expertise that lies outside of government is about far more than just computer coding. For example, to defend the national banking system from cyberattack, a mix of hackers and bankers is better than just bankers or hackers.

These efforts have helped turn Estonia from one of the first victims of a state-level cyberattack, when Russian hackers partially <u>shut down</u> the country in 2007, to perhaps the best-equipped nation in the world to weather one now. Estonia may not have the same capabilities as the NSA and Cyber Command, but it does have deterrence by denial and an involved populace -- giving it arguably better cybersecurity than the United States.

Conclusions: Reaching Real (Cyber) Security

The overall lesson from Cold War deterrence is that the most dangerous period was when both the new technology and the new competition were not well understood -- which made <u>bluster</u> and <u>escalation</u> seemingly easy remedies to complex problems. Fortunately, <u>cooler heads prevailed</u> and the U.S. built up a system that delivered actual deterrence.

Today, we have a similar choice when it comes to the risks of digital attack and the conversation we have about how to face them. The United States can build a new set of approaches designed to deliver true cybersecurity, aiming to both better protect ourselves while reshaping adversary attitudes and options. Or, we can keep talking tough and simple about cyber deterrence, and continue to be victims.

50

Mr. HURD. Thank you, Mr. Singer.

I would now like to recognize Mr. DeSantis for 5 minutes of questioning.

Mr. DESANTIS. Thank you, Mr. Chairman.

General Alexander, how do you view the distinction, if you think there's one, between the threat from state-sanctioned cyber attacks versus nonstate actors who are trying to attack us in cyberspace?

Mr. ALEXANDER. I would not make a distinction based on the impact to our Nation. And I think that's an extremely important question you bring out, because it really says: What's the role of government in protecting this country. And it doesn't matter who takes down the financial sector, the energy sector, the healthcare sector. If it goes down, that's critical to our Nation.

So the consequence and the approach in our strategy has to discuss both. We learned that in 9/11. While there may not be direct ties to this or direct linkage back, I think that's the approach that we should take—look at what the impact to the Nation would be.

Mr. DESANTIS. And I agree with that in terms of trying to prevent that. How, though, if there is a successful attack, how do you then respond if there are, in fact, nonstate actors who are responsible? After 9/11, I think that's actually a good framework to think about it, the policy was, look, if you're a state actor, you may not have committed the attack, but if you're harboring terrorists who are going it, we're going to hold you liable.

Does that same framework, will that work in cyberspace? Because it would seem to be difficult that a government would be able to have a handle on everybody who's operating in cyberspace.

Mr. ALEXANDER. Right. So you've asked a great question in that, because it also gets you back to our strategy. And the strategy can't be: What are we going to do after an attack? It's really what you're hitting on, is we can't afford to allow that kind of attack to occur. And so what it really does is it says we're going to shape our strategy on preventing, not on forensics.

Now, forensics are important, we do have to go through, but if everything is based on after-the-fact forensics, then you're already lost something. And what you're really getting to is we need a defensive strategy that stops that from happening.

And I would take it one step further. We look at the theft of intellectual property, the greatest transfer of wealth in history. That's taking our future away from us. How do we defend against that? And I believe that's where government and industry need to work together.

I like Peter's approach about working together with industry. We need to make a more secure cyberspace. And all the rules that we could put in with State, with DOD, but it has to be a linkage to the commercial side. They own the vast majority of the networks.

Mr. DESANTIS. Mr. Kanuck, you talked about how people in cyberspace could be doing espionage, typical things that governments do. They could also be doing it, which would be considered more of an attack along the lines of an act of war.

So do we have the forensic ability to determine whether a particular measure was meant or compromise was an attack versus a form of espionage, and how does that impact our ability to calibrate our response?

Mr. KANUCK. In response to particular incidents, there are usually ad hoc investigations dealing with the particular circumstances. It is very difficult to divine the intentions of would be adversaries or actors in specific instances. Often you might derive that information from other sources of information, intelligence collection and other areas, to know what actors' objectives may have been. Simply looking from the forensic data, if you are able to see what was exfiltrated and where it went and how it was later used, that may give you a sense of the objectives.

I will simply offer that in the real-time context of an ongoing incident, where you would want to be responding in a policy or military sense in real time, that will be a very high challenge for real-time attribution, and to motivation as well. If you are permitting policy responses days, weeks, months later when you do have a higher degree of attribution, that may be possible, but it is not a certainly that you always know who did it and why.

Mr. DESANTIS. Great.

Mr. Singer, we're hearing more about nonstate actors, terrorist groups, criminal groups using sophisticated toolkits to launch cyber attacks. So, first of all, are sophisticated cyber capabilities finding their way to less sophisticated actors? Are we seeing evidence of that?

Mr. SINGER. Yes, they are. They proliferate. However, I think we still need to recognize that states are the big dog in this, both because of their higher technical capability, so, for example, ISIS was mentioned, lethal group in lots of different ways, but their cyber capability pales compared to China or Russia.

The second is the scale that a state can bring to the problem. So it's not just sophistication. It's the ability to mobilize thousands, tens of thousands or hundreds of thousands of people in the community if you are carrying out an attack.

States are a fundamentally different challenge here than nonstate actors. Fortunately, on the good side, states have interests, and so they can be deferred in a different way than many nonstate actors can't, so we shouldn't bundle them together.

Mr. DESANTIS. Thanks. My time has expired, and I yield back.

Mr. HURD. General Alexander, do you want to answer that?

Mr. ALEXANDER. Yeah, Mr. Chairman. I would recommend, based on what Chairman DeSantis brought up, that the committee might consider getting a briefing or a demonstration of the dark Web. It answers the question that you were just asking: What's available for hackers out there, what do they do to buy it, and how are they getting their materials? And there are companies that have some of these demonstrations that I think you would find extremely informative on just that question: How is it proliferating?

Mr. HURD. Thank you, General.

And we're going to recognize Ms. Kelly for her 5 minutes of questions, and then we'll go into recess for votes.

Ms. KELLY. Thank you, Mr. Chairman.

Mr. Singer, in a December 2015 article for Foreign Policy magazine's Web site, you said that government strategies for responding to cyber threats is based on assumptions and plans made for the cold war threats that are 30, 40, 50 years old. Is that accurate?

Mr. SINGER. Yes.

Ms. KELLY. Okay.

Deputy Assistant Secretary Hughes, during the cold war, our strategy of mutually assured destruction was based on the fact that we could tell instantly if the Soviets fired an intercontinental missile. Is that correct?

Mr. HUGHES. Yes.

Ms. KELLY. Is it equally obvious to figure out where a cyber attack originates?

Mr. HUGHES. I think, as Mr. Kanuck said, there's many factors that go into that attribution and determination. So I'd say it's probably not as instantaneous as it was during the cold war.

Ms. KELLY. And why do you think that is? Just because there are so many factors?

Mr. HUGHES. The number of factors, there's a number of actors, diverse operators on the Internet, makes it extremely difficult.

Ms. KELLY. Okay. Thank you.

Mr. Singer, unlike during the cold war, you said, when considering responses to a cyber attack, and I quote, "the defender's best move may well not be to strike back as rapidly as possible, but to show no outside awareness of the ongoing attack."

Deputy Assistant Secretary Hughes, why might the U.S. choose not to respond to a cyber attack?

Mr. HUGHES. Well, ma'am, I think it goes to points that my colleague Mr. Painter made in terms of what our response might be. I think there's a number of factors from foreign policy implications and the like that we want to make a determination on response on a case-by-case basis.

Ms. KELLY. So the main question of this hearing is, when do we strike back against an adversary for a malicious cyber attack? Taking it one step further, when do we respond with not just a cyber attack of our own, but possibly missiles and tanks?

Mr. Singer, you said that we need to think differently about our response to cyber attacks, and I was trying to write down everything you said. You talked about deter through diversity, sanctions, indictments, being creative and flexible, maybe revealing finances of our enemy. Any other strategies you want to add? You talked about HR and talents to bring aboard.

Mr. SINGER. There's a whole series of things, but I think the key here is to recognize, when we're talking about the attacks, there is a wide array of them, so the attack on us might be anything from intellectual property theft to espionage, stealing of a state secret, to our feared scenario of something that causes mass loss of life.

The first two, traditionally, have not been defined as acts of war. The third may meet that definition. And then in no way, shape, or form would we want to limit ourselves to a merely cyber response to it. We would want to have all the tools there.

The other issue here is the timing. Part of why you may choose to delay your response is not just the normative questions. It's to complicate the attacker's job. If you know that they're inside your system, you can then observe them, steer them into areas where they can't cause harm.

The bottom line here is that we're going to need a very creative and diverse strategy, and the old kind of cold war model of whacking back if they hack us just won't be successful. It won't deliver actual cybersecurity.

Ms. KELLY. Thank you.

Mr. Hughes and Mr. Painter, how do you respond?

Mr. PAINTER. I'd say a couple of things. First of all—and this also goes to Chairman DeSantis' question—we do have a range of tools in our toolkit. So, yes, hacking or using cyber offensive operations could be one. Using kinetic operations may be another, depending on what the incident is. We said in our international strategy in cyberspace back in 2011, we have the full range of tools we'll use if the incident is significant enough, including diplomatic, including economic, including cyber tools, including kinetic tools in appropriate circumstances. We'll try to exhaust the law enforcement and network security tool first.

I also quite agree that part of this is—I'd push back against the view that we are looking at this from a nuclear perspective or one that's from 50 years ago. I think one of the things we've been doing and spending a lot of time on is looking at this whole-of-government approach where we're really looking at new capabilities, new tools, making sure we're inculcating this throughout not just our government, but NATO was mentioned, making sure that NATO has this as part of their strategic concept, making sure that other countries understand this and we have more of a collective defense.

That's exactly what we're trying to do. And when you're talking about the criminal threat, I agree with General Alexander that it's not—you know, you look at the effects. The effects might be the same, but the tools you use to respond might be different. If it's a nation-state, you have certain tools. It it's a criminal group, you might be using law enforcement investigatory tools.

Ms. KELLY. Do you have anything much different, because my time is running out? Is there anything else?

Mr. HUGHES. No, I think Chris hit it right on the head. There's a diverse way that we can respond, and we need to bring all those to bear for each event.

Ms. KELLY. Thank you.

Mr. HURD. So votes have been called, so the chair is going to declare a recess until immediately following the last vote.

[recess.]

Mr. HURD. The Committees on Information Technology and National Security will come to order. Again, for the record, General Alexander had to depart for a prior engagement.

And now I would like to call on the ranking member of the National Security Subcommittee, Mr. Lynch, for his round of questions.

Mr. LYNCH. Thank you very much, Mr. Chairman.

And, again, I thank the witnesses.

Mr. Singer, in your written testimony for today's hearing, one of the ways in which you indicate the United States could strengthen its cybersecurity protocols is through the continued development of international norms of conduct between nation-states. And I think that's correct. But I do know that we have had a recent problem with the SWIFT network, which is an international banking network that is critical to our economy and especially to our international finance community.

The difficulty there is that we've had evidence that there were several possible points of vulnerability, one being the Bangladeshi bank that was the principal bank, but also we've got cooperation by the Federal Reserve Bank of New York in forwarding $81 million to a Philippine casino. And so these people actually got away with this. This is $81 million through the SWIFT network that was actually achieved by the hackers.

I know they tried to transfer about $1.8 billion. They got way with $81 million. Still, it's very concerning because of the importance of the SWIFT network.

And I'm just wondering, if you go by the theory that we're only as strong as our weakest link, there are some suspect practices in Bangladesh and in the Philippines that people think may have contributed to that hack. And in addition, I think there are a dozen banks that have been now identified and had contact with FireEye, which is the security firm that was involved at the Bangladesh central bank.

So all of the banks are southeastern banks, Southeast Asia. None of the banks, except for the Fed, and apparently they have the right codes and the right protocols from the Bangladesh central bank, but no banks in the United States, no banks in Western Europe. The implication could be that those banks in Southeast Asia did not have the firewalls, did not have the cybersecurity systems that the European banks and U.S. banks have.

So how do we approach that? Especially, I mean, you could take an approach that people are not allowed to participate if they don't have a robust cybersecurity system in place. But that would put a lot of developing countries—Nigeria, perfect example, growing economy—that would shut a lot of people out from the international banking communities.

So it presents difficulties. But the size of these hacks, these breaches, is problematic, so we've got to do something. I was just wondering if you had any thoughts since you raised it in your written testimony.

Mr. SINGER. I'd raise three things.

First, I agree completely with you that the attack on the SWIFT system is significant to the U.S. because of what it means, not just for us, but the global financial system. So the first issue is, at least from colleagues in that world, they are not yet satisfied that the fixes that are needed to be made, that the assurance that these kind of breaches can't happen again, they haven't received it in sort of a third-party validated manner. The confidence in the system isn't there. So we need to focus on how do we restore confidence in the system that these fixes have been made.

Second is the idea of norm building. Norm building is not just identifying what kind of attacks should or shouldn't be allowed to happen. It's also for us to figure out identifying sorts of targets that everyone can agree should be off limits. So, for example, this is an area of concord that we might have with a China, with a Russia, and the like, that attacks on the targets may not be militarily significant, but they harm us all. So the norm building is going to have to be—the difference with cold war where any kind of target was allowed, but the attack didn't happen, now we now have lots of different attacks, but it's focusing on which targets are allowed.

The third category is actually linked to a different incident, which we haven't talked about, but I think is crucial to norm building, essentially, the failure of the U.S. and the international community to respond to the December hack of the Ukrainian power grid.

This is the first proven takedown of this kind. It's the long-discussed nightmare scenario. It's a violation of a widely agreed norm not to target civilian infrastructure with the intent to cause widespread and disproportionate damage. And yet, in the story of action and consequence, we had action. So far we've had no consequence.

So if we're talking about norm building, SWIFT is a great example, but the Ukraine one, I think, is even more important for us to wrestle with.

Mr. LYNCH. That's great.

I'm not sure, if Mr. Painter, you have anything you would like to add?

Mr. PAINTER. Yeah, if I could.

Mr. LYNCH. Or Mr. Kanuck or Mr. Hughes.

Mr. PAINTER. Part of the solution to this is the long-term norm building. And this is something we've undertaken and, frankly, as I've said we've led on. And the idea is, there was this very high level of cyber war, which we don't see and, frankly, don't see every day, but there's a lot of conduct we see below that level. And we've made a lot of progress in a short time in not only getting countries that are like-minded to agree, but also getting China and Russia, for instance, to agree.

And the norms we've been promoting are, for instance, don't attack the critical infrastructure of another country absent wartime that provide services to the public, don't attack certs, don't attack the computer emergency response teams. Don't use them for bad, use them for defensive purposes. And an expectation that you if you get a request from another state and there's malicious code coming or activity coming from that state, that you're going to mitigate it through technical or law enforcement means. And then, finally, don't steal the intellectual property using cyber means of another country for your commercial benefit.

And that's new, and we're promoting that, and that's some of the stuff we have been doing in the G–20. If you look at literally every time the President has a meeting with a foreign leader, every single time, and the Nordic summit is an example, the Modi visit just recently is another, you'll see a big statement on cyber, including these norms. That's a real priority.

Mr. LYNCH. Yeah. Thank you.

Mr. HURD. I'd like to recognize Mr. Russell for 5 minutes.

Mr. RUSSELL. Thank you, Mr. Chairman.

And, gentlemen, thank you for being here. It's been a really insightful discussion. And I guess what was mentioned earlier by General Alexander, I believe, talking about the rise of ransomware and these bitcoin hostage-taking of servers in businesses, we see it all the way down to small businesses, as a preferred method, too difficult to fight, not a big enough dollar amount to matter, and they're raking the public for millions of dollars.

Could you speak to that a little bit? And then I've got another line that I'd like to discuss after that. Whoever would like to take that, or anyone that wants to comment on that.

Mr. KANUCK. I think one of the issues you point to is the magnitude of specific incidents. And during my work at ODNI, and certainly in some of the Director Clapper's testimony in the past, he's talked about the cumulative effect of low to moderate level attacks that are already compromising U.S. economic competitiveness and national security. So I would simply draw attention to that.

It's analytically recognized that the cumulative impact can be very significant even if individual events are not that large. And then that becomes a policy response or a legislative or regulatory issue for policy determinations of how and when to respond. But analytically speaking, the mere fact that you're not seeing singular gigantic events should not put anyone at ease about the problem, because the cumulative effects are very, very significant and deleterious.

Mr. RUSSELL. And I'm not even sure that it's due to these hostile nation militaries. I've actually had constituents that have, you know, they've been pirated. Their servers have been frozen. We've seen things like this.

Mr. Singer, and then you, Mr. Painter. Thank you.

Mr. SINGER. I would agree completely. And it points, again, to the value of the resilience node and the strategy where the way to mitigate these attacks is to spread best practices and, second, to help spur on the development of the cyber insurance industry that both backstops these victims, but also help incentivize them to have the best practices that avoid it.

Second, it's a great example of how it points to the value of an offensive hit back within the cyber realm wouldn't do anything to solve this problem. This is why you have to have a very diverse strategy.

Mr. RUSSELL. Yeah. I agree with that.

Mr. Painter.

Mr. PAINTER. And I would say three things.

One, hardening the targets, just to emphasize hardening the targets, which is a difficult job, but so important. And our colleagues from DHS who are not here can speak to that especially, but also the private sector.

The second is, this is an evolution of a threat we've seen before. I remember a case when I was at Justice where then-Mayor Bloomberg—he wasn't mayor then—when Bloomberg had his business, someone hacked into his information. They threatened to expose all of it if he didn't pay them ransom. And he cooperated with the FBI, and they arrested the guy.

So this is the newest iteration of that kind of a threat, and it certainly has very damaging characteristics. But one thing—and, again I'd defer to my Justice colleagues on this—that we did in the fraud cases, where you had lots of small frauds, and they end up sometimes being the same actors, if you look at how to aggregate that, you share intelligence, so you look at the actors and you go after the actors.

Mr. RUSSELL. Well, and it seems to me—and, Mr. Singer, you had made mention of best practices and things—there's just some basic things that could be done. One, report it to the FBI. It might seem insignificant to them, to the business, but it is important in a collective thing. And then the other thing, routine backups, changes, all of that, things that we kind of take for granted.

Really, we're looking at a sphere of technology not unlike 100 years ago in the electronic warfare sphere. We were using telegraphs, then we were using wireless, then we had towers in communication and in satellite, and we saw the maturation of electronic warfare.

And I would argue that a lot of our systems that we have in place today with regard to electronic warfare is the same sphere for cyber attack. They use the same power sources, the same type of infrastructure to spread out and branch even with the digital. I see it very much like that, electronic warfare, a war in the shadows.

Isn't there a way that we could also do strike-back attack in that war on the shadows that's not public? I leave that with whoever wants to answer that.

Mr. HUGHES. I guess the one comment I would make to that is we've tried actually do the opposite of that through the release of our most recent strategy and try to normalize activities in cyber so it is out of the shadows, so there's more transparency around what we're doing and a better understanding both from our allies, the American people, as well as our adversaries as to what your intentions are.

I think it's when folks view it as being in the shadows that there's more question about what we're doing to respond to malicious activity. So I this I we're trying to normalize activities in the domain and not make it more classified.

Mr. KANUCK. I think Mr. Hughes raises an important point about increasing transparency. Clearly, certain intelligence activities, to include covert action, may have their place at certain times and in certain instances, but normalizing and increasing transparency could be greatly helpful.

And I offer that what any nation would choose to do sets precedents that are very difficult to prevent other nations from copying in the future. So the question would have to be asked, would you want that to be the rule that all countries obeyed of operating on partial or medium confidence attribution to be taking clandestine action with deleterious effects?

That could be a very dangerous environment if everyone is not acting with very, very high standards of attribution and preventing collateral damage.

Mr. PAINTER. And if I may very quickly, I think, we can't discuss it in this environment, because it's a classified Presidential directive, but we can say there is a Presidential directive that deals with this. And it's important for countries to have doctrine around this, so there is that kind of predictability that Sean talked about.

And our doctrine does two things. One, it makes sure that everything is integrated. We're not just thinking about these things separately, but we're integrating all our capabilities and all of the different equities involved. And, two, that we're going to favor network security and law enforcement as our first lines of defense and then look at other tools after that.

Mr. RUSSELL. And as I close, Mr. Chairman, thank you for your indulgence. I guess there's a part of me and the warrior in me, do you want to answer a Sony attack with a Stuxnet or do you want to wish that you had good practices and everybody cooperates? I personally think there has to be a balance of both. If we show ourselves weak, this problem is only going to grow.

And thank you, Mr. Chairman. I yield back.

Mr. HURD. The gentleman from California, Mr. Lieu, you're recognized.

Mr. LIEU. Thank you, Mr. Chair.

Mr. Hughes, thank you for your public service. I have some questions for you.

Earlier this year, Defense Secretary Carter stated that encryption was absolutely critical to the Department of Defense in terms of protecting cybersecurity. Would you agree with that?

Mr. HUGHES. Yeah. I mean, Department of Defense systems rely on encryption for our communication out in the field and with our partners. Absolutely.

Mr. LIEU. He also stated that he opposed back doors that would weaken encryption. Do you agree with that as well?

Mr. HUGHES. I would support the Secretary's position for the Department.

Mr. LIEU. And I just want to make sure, the Department's view is that we need to move to stronger encryption, not weaker encryption. Is that correct?

Mr. HUGHES. I support the Secretary's position on encryption.

Mr. LIEU. Thank you.

So now I would like to ask you, in your job, do you deal with telephone networks' communications as part of what you deal with in your role in terms of cybersecurity?

Mr. HUGHES. So I think there's collaborations between what my office does for operational oversight, international partnerships, and interagency collaboration of cyber policy and what the DOD CIO does from oversight from a network security and telephony perspective. My office, per se, does not cover telephony protocols or any of the technical specifics.

Mr. LIEU. Okay. Earlier this year it was revealed there was a flaw known as the Signaling System No. 7 flaw in our telephone networks. And as I understand it, decades ago when they set up these networks, and let's say you had to make a call to Africa, the U.S. network would hand off to a European network or hand off to the African network. And it was assumed that these networks would be trusted. It turns out that some of these networks are owned by foreign adversaries like Russia or Iran or criminal syndicates related to these foreign adversaries.

Have you looked at that issue at all?

Mr. HUGHES. I'd have to take that question for the record. It's not something that my office in particular has looked at.

Mr. LIEU. Who in the DOD would be looking at that issue?

Mr. HUGHES. I'd have to take that for the record. I would assume the DOD CIO would look into that, but I would have to get back to you on that.

Mr. LIEU. If you could, that would be great. Because, as I understand it, if a foreign government exploits this SS7 flaw, which any foreign government that has a telephone network can, it then allows them to listen in on the telephone conversations of anybody's cell phone just knowing that cell phone number, track their movements, and get their text messages.

It always struck me as odd when we go on these codels abroad, we get all these briefings on don't take your smartphones, have these protections, make sure you follow these cybersecurity hygiene tips when you're in these foreign countries, when it turns out these foreign countries can just listen in on our phone conversations knowing our cell phone number right here in the United States.

So if we could get some information back on that and whether the problem has been fixed, it would be helpful.

Mr. LIEU. And then I have some questions related to the Obama administration's new Cybersecurity Workforce Strategy that was announced yesterday. One of the proposals is to increase funding and salaries to recruit and retain talented cyber professionals.

So the question for you, Mr. Hughes, as well as you, Mr. Painter, I'd like to know what is the issue with that, how important is it? And second, what is your sort of view on your ability to retain people once you get them in the cybersecurity field?

Mr. HUGHES. So I can speak to the Secretary's Force of the Future initiatives around the Department of Defense. I'm not familiar with the specific program that the administration just released writ large.

Specific to Department of Defense, we're always looking at novel ways to bring in and recruit and retain more talented professionals across a variety of domains. We understand the acute challenges of retaining our highly trained and skilled personnel that operate on the cyber systems.

And so the Secretary's Force of the Future initiative is looking at a variety of different ways to have more permeability between private sector and government service, as well as different ways to bring in folks to serve in different positions, both military and civilian.

Mr. LIEU. Thank you.

Mr. PAINTER. And I would say, yes, this is part of the larger administration attempt to really bolster our cybersecurity. One of the problems we face, not as much in my shop because I'm a policy shop, but certainly throughout the government, is finding qualified people who do cybersecurity work. Competing with the private sector. It's still a fairly small pool. I'd say that there are schools, and we have been working with schools to get programs to have more people dealing with this.

I should say that I was a 9-year resident of your district, and I suspect that many of them live in your district, and I do miss it every day. So if you can convince them to come out here, that would be great.

Mr. LIEU. Thank you.

Thank you. I yield back.

Mr. HURD. Mr. Hice from Georgia is recognized for 5 minutes.

Mr. HICE. Thank you, Mr. Chairman.

I want to begin with you, Mr. Hughes, but if others of you have some input, feel free to jump in here. But what are the factors that define a cyber act of war as opposed to a cyber attack?

Mr. HUGHES. So, again, as I mentioned in my opening statement, cyber incidents are reviewed on a case-by-case basis. We take into account loss of life, injury to person, destruction of property, and the national security leadership, and the President will make the determination if it's an armed attack. But I would defer to Mr. Painter for a more thorough——

Mr. PAINTER. Yeah, I echo that completely. I think it's an effects-based test, just like it is in the physical world. So we are not using a separate test for the physical.

Mr. HICE. So at what point do we—what are the rules of engagement that would determine a response, be it a cyber response or kinetic?

Mr. HUGHES. Again, not to sound cliche, but, again, it will be on a case-by-case basis. We will evaluate each incident on its merits and make a determination, again, through a whole-of-government collaboration, on what the response might be.

Mr. HICE. So who makes that decision? Is it the President alone or are there multiple agencies or representatives from the agencies that would be involved?

Mr. HUGHES. The national security leadership, in conjunction with the President, make that determination.

Mr. PAINTER. But I would say that, as we look at these, there are a range of different activities. And you use the term cyber warfare, but the question often is what constitutes an armed attack under international law that would then give a right to self-defense. But even if it's below that threshold, we still have a way—there's a number of ways to respond. It could be kinetic. It could be through cyber means. It could be through economic means and sanctions. It could be through diplomacy. It could be through indictments and law enforcement actions.

And what we have done, and this is one of the things, having tracked this for so long, I've seen as a real change and a really beneficial change, is there is a very, very strong interagency process that as we're looking at these threats—I mean, Aaron and I, in particular, we talk all the time—but all the different interagency colleagues do talk about these threats, talk about possible responses.

In the end, it's up to the National Security Staff and the President, but we look at all these different opportunities. If it's a criminal matter, Justice will take it, for instance. So we'll look at our tools.

Mr. HICE. I'm concerned with the lack of clarity on this and the bureaucratic, multilayered involvement to make a decision. And now we have Cyber Command in Fort Gordon.

If CYBERCOM were elevated to a full combatant command, would that help?

Mr. HUGHES. I think we're always looking at ways to make the military establishment more efficient and effective. I wouldn't say that elevation of Cyber Command in and of itself would help in the determination of a cyber incident being an armed attack versus other types of malicious activity.

Mr. HICE. Mr. Singer.

Mr. SINGER. To weigh in from outside of government, essentially, in defining whether it's a war or not, many of the same measures would be used, whatever the means, cyber or physical. To put it bluntly, it is throughout history it's decided by does it combine a political intent and mass violence of some kind, physical violence, death, injury.

So, as an example, there are cyber attacks that steal secrets, they are incredibly vexing, but no Nation has ever gone to war over just because their secrets are stolen. The judgment, though, is a political judgment on when it's an act of war. And my hope is, and this is the value of this hearing, that it's not just the President or the NSC, but it's also Congress traditionally has decided when the U.S. is at war or not.

Mr. HICE. Well, yes, to some extent. But let's go down that path a little bit further then. Can a member of NATO invoke Article 5 for a cyber attack?

Mr. PAINTER. Yes, they can. In fact, there's been a lot of activity in NATO since 2012. Cyber is part of NATO's operating construct. We just had a leaders-level meeting for NATO where they agreed, among other things—they previously agreed that international law applies, including the Law of Armed Conflict. They are doing cyber strategies that Aaron can talk more to. But one of the things that was agreed to back in, I think it was 2014, is that cyber could qualify under Article 5.

Mr. HICE. Okay. Well, then, let me ask this. Does NATO have a definition of what constitutes a cyber attack, seeing that we don't?

Mr. PAINTER. First, I think it's not true that we don't have a definition. We just talked about what would qualify and the factors you would use.

I would have to go back and look at NATO's doctrine, but I think they have a lot of focus on this, they understand the risks out there, and they are building the capability.

Mr. HICE. All right. Well, our definition was not clearly communicated to me. It was going to be left up to the President and others based on certain factors and somewhere they're going to make a decision.

But I assume my time has expired. Mr. Chairman, I thank you for your indulgence. I yield back.

Mr. HURD. The gentleman from Iowa. Mr. Blum, you are recognized for 5 minutes.

Mr. BLUM. Thank you, Mr. Chairman. I appreciate it.

And thank you to our witnesses today for providing us some insights into this growing problem of cybersecurity.

I come from the private sector. I've been operating in the private sector my entire career. So I would like to chat a little bit about China and the United States private sector. And while most of my questions would be toward Mr. Painter from the State Department, anyone else feel free to jump in.

Mr. Painter, the State Department's Overseas Security Advisory Council, OSAC, recently concluded that, despite media's reporting that Chinese cyber attacks are decreasing, cases of a Chinese espionage campaign against the U.S. private sector are ongoing. Which sectors, Mr. Painter, do you think are most at risk for these Chinese cyber attacks?

Mr. PAINTER. Look, I think the DNI has talked about this, and we continue to see intrusions in the systems, both government systems and private sector systems, for espionage purposes.

What we agreed to with China, which was significant, is that they would not break into private sector systems to steal intellectual property or trade secrets or business or proprietary information for the purposes of benefiting their commercial sector.

On that, we have been pushing them very hard. There's a number of ways we have been doing that. It was really a remarkable fact that they came to that agreement when President Xi was here. And we said we are going to hold them accountable. We are still going to use all the tools we have.

And the jury is still out. I think Admiral Rogers recently testified, saying we are watching closely. But the jury is still out.

Mr. BLUM. Any other comments on that question?

Mr. KANUCK. Again, I left government on May 9 of this year, but up until that point, I would concur with what Chris has just said. Having been the office that was charged with making those determinations on behalf of the U.S. Government, the jury is still out or was as of May 9.

And I would just offer two other considerations that one has to think about, and I mentioned this in my written statement. Modus operandis may change, so behavioral patterns may change. And the question of volume or quantity versus rate of success and quality of foreign activities is something that needs to be considered.

So I would recommend that if that is an issue that is of interest to you, sir, that's probably better for closed hearings with my colleagues or others from the intelligence agencies in the future. But asking what the current impacts are and what, if anything, has changed and metrics, that kind of attribution analysis is very, very difficult and you quickly get into classified discussions. But it's a worthwhile question and one we grappled with for my 5 years at ODNI.

Mr. BLUM. Mr. Singer.

Mr. SINGER. If I understood your question, it was in essence who is being targeted, and it's a confluence of two factors. It's, one, what are their national priorities for economic success. To put it another way, what industries do they want to be global leaders. And those are industries that have been most targeted for intellectual property theft in the past. The agreement may change that.

And the second is vulnerabilities, where are the weak links and who are they able to get into, and that, again, points to the value of resilience-based strategy where it's effective be it against the threat of intellectual property theft to the threat from cyberterrorist to China in a military means. Good defense actually is good defense.

Mr. BLUM. Mr. Painter.

Mr. PAINTER. And I would certainly agree with the hardening of the targeted issue, which we've raised a number of times. But I would also say, it's not just the U.S. So, one, the important thing is a lot of other countries have raised this concern. The U.K. has raised it, Germany has raised it, and others. And the G–20 statement that I talked about where there is an affirmation among the leaders of the G–20 that this conduct was impermissible I think is

also important. It sets a metric that we can hold people accountable by.

Mr. BLUM. Relative to China, and since we're talking about cyber
attacks in the private sector, one would think the reason for China
doing this would be economic. But is there any military reason
China would be attacking our private sector? Maybe Mr. Hughes
would have some insight into this.

What are your thoughts? Are these attacks, cyber attacks, mainly private sector economic or are they also military?

Mr. HUGHES. I think they're probably targeting our private sector
companies to enhance their national security apparatus as well. I'm
sure that some of our defense industrial base companies are being
targeted by the Chinese to benefit their military development in
advancement of their technologies.

Mr. BLUM. Mr. Painter, any other insights on that?

Mr. PAINTER. No, I would agree. I would think that you'll see,
just as the DNI set a full spectrum of targets given the information
that's out there.

Mr. BLUM. Have, in fact, China's cyber attacks, the amount of
them, decreased over the last 5 years? Is that a fact?

Mr. HUGHES. I would defer that question to the closed hearing
and to the intelligence community.

Mr. PAINTER. I would agree with that. I think that would be a
ripe subject for the closed hearing.

What I can say is, in terms of the theft of intellectual property
for commercial purposes, as Admiral Rogers said, the jury is still
out on that, and I believe the DNI said that too. But with respect
to any more detail, we can get into that in another setting.

Mr. BLUM. Mr. Singer.

Mr. SINGER. As to the question on the goal of intellectual property theft not just being economic, it definitely has a national security side. And the easy answer to you would be Google images of
F–35 and J–31, and you will see a remarkable similarity between
our most expensive weapons project and their new jet fighter system. And either it's coincidentally they look alike or there's something else going on.

Mr. BLUM. What can Congress do to provide additional deterrence to countries like China? It may be criminal law, for example.
What more can we do? What are your suggestions? And I'm thinking of China specifically here, but it applies to all nations, obviously.

Here's your chance. Here's your chance. Tell us what to do.

Mr. KANUCK. I would offer that this is really an issue of strategic
reality, incentives, disincentives, and consequences. We've talked
about attribution, public attribution, and that there may be no bite
behind the bark. I would offer you have to look at very complex bilateral relationships, certainly if you're looking at United States
and China, but also with other countries, and ask, what would
strategically incentivize or decentivize changes in behavior? Having
served 16 years in the intelligence community, for me it was about
what was actually happening, not what was being said.

And, again, to get at the very particulars of that, about volumes
of activity or impact of activity, that is, again, something I would
say that the current serving members of the intelligence commu-

nity and other executive agencies would be better off discussing in a closed session.

Mr. PAINTER. I would just add that the fact that in this case the President, and at the highest levels of our government, obviously, the President raising this with the President of China as not just an issue of cyber versus cyber, but an issue that affected the over-all relationship, pattern had a big impact.

Mr. BLUM. And if I have time for one more question, Mr. Chairman?

I would just like to ask the panel, has there been any noticeable effect following the Department of Justice 2014 indictment of the PLA officers? Has there been any noticeable effect?

Mr. KANUCK. From my observation, that became a strong topic of discussion between U.S. Government and Chinese Government officials, and I'd defer to my colleagues who are still in government regarding there. And there were also negative ramifications for certain U.S. companies who had business opportunities in China very quickly curtailed.

So it had an economic and business impact on U.S. Entities and it also certainly was a central part of the discussions, of the policy discussions, which are better answered by the policy departments.

Mr. BLUM. Mr. Painter.

Mr. PAINTER. And I'd defer to my colleagues who are not here from the Department of Justice, but I would say that, yes, the dialogue we had with the Chinese about deescalation and norms in cyberspace was suspended—we have now gotten back on another foot on that—which seemed an odd reaction to that.

But, nevertheless, I think it showed that we were serious, certainly, and that when, you know, that combined with the President raising it and the threat of sanctions and other things, I think likely brought the Chinese to the table. But that is more an assessment for others.

Mr. BLUM. Any insights on that, Mr. Hughes?

Mr. HUGHES. Again, I would also defer to the Intel community for a classified assessment and then Department of Justice.

Mr. BLUM. I have no further questions, Mr. Chairman. I yield back the time I do not have.

Mr. HURD. I recognize myself for 5 minutes.

Once again, gentleman, thank you all for being here. Thank you for your patience. You guys are all very influential in keeping us safe, and I appreciate that. Sorry to keep you away from your day jobs too long.

This is a funny topic for me to be the chairman of, considering I spent most of my adult life in the clandestine world, right? But having everyone that has a role in this side by side, there's value to this. And I've taken a lot away from these conversations, so I really appreciate that.

And I have some basic questions. My first question is to everybody. And I don't ask this as a yes-or-no question. It's a really basic question. I'd welcome a little detail.

And I'll start with you, Mr. Hughes. Do the bad guys know what we can do?

Mr. HUGHES. I think, similar to the U.S. national security infrastructure having intelligence agencies, our adversaries are also doing collection against us. In some instances, they are likely tracking our TTPs. So I would assert that they have some idea of our ability to exploit networks and get information, absolutely.

Mr. HURD. Mr. Painter.

Mr. PAINTER. Yeah. I think also there's a benefit in the bad guys knowing what we can do to some extent. I mean, we certainly in, for instance, the criminal law context want to project that there will be consequences for people's actions, so we want that, that we have economic tools we can use, we have other tools we can use. That's part of the deterrence message, is the bad guys knowing, whoever the bad guy might be, what you can do.

And in that, I think, what I have seen personally is that we have made real progress in communicating that. One of the questions was asked earlier about the Bangladeshi situation. Part of this is outside the U.S., which is part of my gig, which is in working with other countries around the world so they have these capabilities too.

Mr. HURD. And, Mr. Kanuck, before you get to that question, I am going to ask you, Mr. Painter, to pick up on something you just said. Ukraine, Romania, Latvia, where are those countries where the legal framework is not there to allow the right kinds of prosecution, because when it's not—we know how many attacks are coming from these different countries—because there's not a legal framework in which for them to get prosecuted or sued.

Where are those places of biggest concern to you? What additional pressures should we be putting on these countries in order to establish that kind of framework?

Mr. PAINTER. So the countries—I mean, I think we've made a lot of progress, especially my Department of Justice colleagues. And one of the things that we do is capacity building. We work with DHS and DOJ. We've done things in Africa, a lot of regional trainings in Africa. We've worked with the EU and others.

We want every country to have strong cybercrime—you know, you can remember the ILOVEYOU virus, where the Philippines didn't have a law to punish this. And now they do. In fact, they've gone through several iterations of that.

So I don't think it's helpful to single out countries and saying you're doing a bad job. I think it's more helpful to help us get in there and work with them, because they also recognize the economic value of this. If they have good cybercrime laws, people want to invest in their economy. You are going to promote innovation.

I think the Budapest Convention, which is the convention—Budapest Cybercrime Convention—the one that we promote around the world, there's been a number of new signatories recently. We're working on getting more in Africa and Asia. Japan joined about a year and a half ago. So that's part of the push.

Now, there are other countries, and this goes to more of the policy issue, like Russia and China, who want a global—a U.N. Convention, and we think that's just wasting time. This is an urgent issue now and countries need to be prepared for it.

Mr. HURD. Mr. Kanuck, not only do the bad guys know what we can do, is there stuff that we should ensure the bad guys know that we can do? And the third piece is, I think the difficulty for a lot of us up here is when you talk what is a digital act of war, the difference between a digital act of war and a gray area and a red line, what does all that mean. And we've had conversations about what is off limits. And I think sometimes part of the public conversation can articulate in a more granule level what is off limits, right?

And, Mr. Singer, you made a great point about the Ukrainian grid attack. If you look at, what is it, the U.N.'s Chapter VII, Article 39, 41, 42, and 51 that talk about those things and where you can defend yourself, the grid is pretty clearly articulated there.

What are some of those other gray areas that we should be exposing? I know there were a lot of questions in there, but you are a smart guy, Mr. Kanuck, you can follow them all.

Mr. KANUCK. I'll do my best to succinctly hit the three. Starting with the ones my colleagues have answered, I think our sophisticated adversaries fully understand the laws of physics, the nature of telecommunications equipment, how electromagnetic spectrum operates, and how software logic code does. They may not know exactly what accesses or we may not exactly what accesses any foreign government may have on any given day or what hardware or software implants may exist. I would liken it to a poker game where everyone knows the cards in the deck, you don't know who is holding which cards in which hand, and those capabilities may be fleeting and influx in any given time.

Secondly, is there a benefit to letting anyone know what we can do in certain instances? Again, while I appreciate clandestine intelligence activities as a 16-year intelligence professional, there may also be reasons in certain cases to declare or show certain capabilities akin to having a standing navy or other armaments that are known for a credible deterrent effect. However, the nature of cyber tools differs in that, if you reveal the particularities of a capability, an adversary may be able to develop countermeasures. So there would be a very sensitive balance there, certainly at least against your most sophisticated adversaries.

Regarding gray areas and red lines, I'd actually like to draw attention to two important points which are on the margins of some of the discussion we've heard today. A lot of discussion has focused on act of war. I actually think that's the wrong focus, as I stated in my written statement.

Most of what we have seen foreign state actors doing has been intentionally designed to operate below the threshold that would trigger Articles 2, 4, Article 51 of the U.N. Charter, or Articles 4, 5 of the Washington Treaty. There is cognizance by many actors to use cyber technologies in an asymmetric coercive tool for influence with the express interest of avoiding military conflict. So that is actually how these weapons and tools are being most utilized.

Mr. HURD. So, Mr. Kanuck, on that, should we be lowering the bar?

Mr. KANUCK. Again, that's a policy decision. I think, for starters, we need to be cognizant of these low- to moderate-level activities and their cumulative effect, like we were discussing earlier with one of your colleagues. Where you actually draw red lines, that is a policy question. I think there are certain casualty levels and certain property damage levels that under an effects-based analysis would constitute an armed attack or an act of war. But that analysis, as has been stated earlier by the executive branch representatives here, is the same that you would use for noncyber modalities.

The last thing I'd like to, if I may just mention, focus is, we need to pay more attention to what will be a problem more and more in the future of attacks on the integrity of data, not on its confidentiality and not on its availability.

Director Clapper has made reference to that in his last two worldwide threat assessments. And I fear, if ransomware is today's news, the future news is going to be integrity, integrity, value of information, not access to it.

Mr. HURD. Turning 10,000 into 1,000 or changing——

Mr. KANUCK. Changing what's seen on an air traffic controller's screen. Changing information in the Twittersphere that will affect investors' actions. Changing the situational awareness that a military commander is seeing. Can you trust the information you're seeing to make actions upon it? That is actually the value of information, and that is what, unfortunately, this conflict space will turn to in the future more and more.

Mr. HURD. And, Mr. Singer, I'm going to add a question to you as well. We talked about effects-based approach. Does an effects-based approach include intended effects or only the actual effects? Can we determine intended effects? Should we be trying to determine intended effects? And should our response be based on the interpretation of what we may think those intended effects are?

Mr. SINGER. So I'll hit that question first, because that's where I do believe the idea that we solely use an effects-based judgment is just not—it's not the way we actually approach it. So to use a noncyber example, a bullet crosses the border into your district and kills someone—effect—but we will judge whether we are at war or it is an act of war from Mexico as to whether it is fired by Mexican Government with intent to kill or is it an accidental discharge, be it by a Mexican government individual. Then we would ask the same question if it was a civilian or not.

Intent does matter. It's one of the things that will be, at least in the political judgement, the kind of political judgment that would be made in the White House, to deliberations in Congress. If it's going to make a declaration of war, it will judge intent as much as effect. The challenge, kind of figuring out the intent, sometimes is going to be unclear.

Mr. HURD. Well, over the last couple of weeks we've learned a whole lot about intent.

Mr. SINGER. Yeah. But the second thing to hit your question about awareness. My belief is that the bad guys have no doubt of our offensive cyber capability. If they had any confusion about it, we had a series of policymaker leaks about the Stuxnet operation, and then we had a massive dump from Edward Snowden, which caused us a lot of problems, but it also showed off we are quite good in this realm.

The challenge is, if you look at the data, there is no evidence that that raised awareness of our offensive capability actually deterred attacks. Overall, data loss to America, in general, citizens, went up 55 percent the year after the Snowden leak. To many of the cases that we've talked about today, whether it's OPM, to ones we haven't talked about, the attacks on the Joint Chiefs' email system, those all happened afterwards.

But that's not to say that deterrence isn't working. So, for example, there's lots of things that a China, a Russia, an Iran could do in this realm. They don't, in large part not merely because of our offensive cyber capability hit back, but because we can hit back in other realms.

Mr. HURD. Well, I'd like to thank the ranking member for indulging me in going over.

And I'm going to ask this last question to all of you all. I recognize the difficulty in the question that I'm asking. It's probably not as difficult for Mr. Singer to answer, and Mr. Kanuck has not been out of government long enough to be able to answer this question easily. You all are involved in policy, you all are involved in operational activity.

But I'm going to ask you, what is the best next action for this House, for Congress on this topic to move the conversation to where we are having a whole-of-government response or improving a whole-of-government response? You know, not the end goal, right? What's the next step? What would you all like to see this legislative body do?

And you don't need to take forever. We've already run out of time.

But, Mr. Singer, I think it's going to be easiest for you to answer this question. So let's start with you and go in reverse order.

And, Mr. Hughes, you get to have the last word.

Mr. SINGER. I'll just hit, again, the written testimony points, particularly about how do we build up our resilience. And there's a series of things that Congress could do, and some of they are quite as simple as, for example, holding a hearing on the cybersecurity insurance industry and how could we bolster it, to there's actual small step mechanisms that could help it go on, to the examples of are there organizations that could be created and the like.

Maybe to sum it up, the question for the Congress is, we know there's a series of best practices out there in private sector and government. How do you help aid their spread and/or where the executive branch has made a commitment to implement them, how do you hold their feet to the fire to ensure that they are actually doing it, particularly across another administration?

Mr. HURD. And we've got the bipartisan part down in your testimony. I think this is one of the things that has been great about this committee.

Mr. Kanuck.

Mr. KANUCK. It's been mentioned by a couple of my colleagues already, but I want to fully add my support to the discussion about resilience, and as one aspect of that, the growing insurance market in this space. When we did our analytic exchanges and outreaches we quickly learned from my old office that resiliency was a necessary component for policy options. If you are not safe, you will be restricted in what you can be doing offensively, defensively, and otherwise.

I'd also like to add, if we're talking from a legislative perspective, I do believe that Congress can have an impact on the Federal workforce. And as a couple of my concluding statements in my written statement said, this is a qualitative not a quantitative game. Cyber expertise is about having the highest level of competence.

The greatest breakthroughs in information technology have not been because there were a thousand people in the room. The greatest breakthroughs in encryption, in hardware, in software have been by small entities. We need to ensure that some of those cyber Olympians are working in the Federal workforce and stay there.

Mr. PAINTER. Amen.

Mr. KANUCK. My last comment will be, it's wrong to think about this as cybersecurity. There is no solution for perfect cybersecurity if you are up against determined, well-resourced adversaries. This is about risk management and risk mediation. The future discussions would be most served for the public good if they were about a cyber risk discussion, or even better, information risk, to include integrity concerns.

Shifting that intellectual framework to information risk will help you a long way towards addressing some of the issues that this panel has raised today.

Mr. HURD. Thank you.

Mr. KANUCK. Thank you.

Mr. HURD. Mr. Painter.

Mr. PAINTER. So I think the number one thing, and given my experience, is to maintain the momentum and the focus on this issue and the education on this issue.

Look, even 5 or 6 years ago, at the end of the Bush administration, there was a conference of national cyber initiatives. Back in 2003, we had a cybersecurity strategy that became shelfwear, because people at the time weren't ready to deal with it.

I think now we're in a different place, but I think it needs to be made a priority and continue to be a priority not just for this administration, but whoever the next administration is. Now, I think we're in good shape there, because I think now, because there are hearings like this and your Senate colleagues in SFRC, I've testified before them, we've done a report to Congress about all of our activities across the board in cyber, including throughout the different range, I think that's all important. But the focus really needs to continue on this and be seen as a priority.

Five years ago, when my office was created at the State Department, there was no real cyber diplomacy program. We now have 22, I think, countries around the world that have counterparts to me that didn't exist, where we can actually not just have dialogues about policy, but when we have an attack like these denial-of-service attacks against financial institutions, I can reach out to counterparts and I can say: Look, this is important. This is not just the normal technical issue. So that's important.

What I'd say we don't need from my Department, because we really crosscut among all the different parts of our Department, is I know there is some proposed legislation to kind of stovepipe this issue and put it into one particular chain and then create more bureaucracy, in my opinion. I'd say that's not helpful to us. What we really need is to be able to mainstream this throughout the Department and really throughout our foreign policy.

Mr. HURD. Mr. Hughes, you get the last words. No pressure.

Mr. HUGHES. Well, first and foremost, as my panelists have said, continue the dialogue. I think awareness across the United States and the American people of cyber threats and vulnerabilities is important. The adversaries aren't using sophisticated tactics to steal data, they're using the low-hanging fruit, and there's such a lack of basic hygiene that they don't need to resort to nation-state level capabilities to steal information.

So continuing the dialogue and awareness is important, because the interdependencies between government networks, private sector networks, foreign entities, I mean, we are all so intertwined that a vulnerability in one can lead to a vulnerability for all.

And then, tactically, I would second, again, what Mr. Kanuck said in terms of workforce—workforce improvements, workforce management. I know the most recent NDAA provided the Department of Defense a little bit more flexibility with the cyber excepted service provisions. We plan to take advantage of that to improve our ability to hire and retain talented cyber professionals.

Mr. HURD. Excellent.

Mr. PAINTER. I would just like to add that also, I want to thank Congress for the recent cyber information-sharing legislation. That has helped.

Mr. HURD. You're welcome.

Without objection, I'd like to enter my full opening remarks for the record.

So ordered.

And I would like to thank our witnesses today for taking the time to appear before us. This is a very important conversation that needs to continue.

And if there's no further business, without objection, the subcommittees stand adjourned.

[Whereupon, at 3:43 p.m., the subcommittees were adjourned.]